Developing a Lean Workforce

This Book Belongs

Developing a Lean Workforce

A Guide for Human Resources, Plant Managers, and Lean Coordinators

CHRIS HARRIS AND RICK HARRIS

Productivity *Press*

New York

Most Productivity Press books are available at quantity discounts when purchased
in bulk. For more information, contact our Customer Service Department (888-319-
5852). Address all other inquires to:

Productivity Press
444 Park Avenue South, 7th floor
New York, NY 10016
United States of America
Telephone: 212-686-5900
Fax: 212-686-5411
E-mail: info@productivitypress.com

Library of Congress Cataloging-in-Publication Data

Harris, Chris.
    Developing a lean workforce : a guide for human resources, plant
managers, and lean coordinators / Chris Harris and Rick Harris.
        p. cm.
    Includes index.
    ISBN 978-1-56327-348-3 (alk. paper)
        1. Personnel management–Management.   2. Employees–
Training of.   3. Facility management.   4. Organizational effectiveness.   I.
Harris, Rick.   II. Title.
    HF5549.H33818   2007
    658.3'01–dc22

                                                                2006102937

11 10 09 08 07   5   4   3   2   1

With gratitude to my wife Joie; without her love and support this book would not have been possible. I would also like to thank my parents for a lifetime of opportunities and encouragement. Finally, I owe a word of thanks to the faculty of the Falls School of Business at Anderson University in Anderson, Indiana, who helped shape the theoretical basis for my work, and to the clients whose lean implementation has helped turn theory into practice and has allowed us to keep learning.

Chris Harris

With gratitude to my wife Ann, because without her belief in me and her enduring love, none of this would have been possible. Thanks also to my sons Christopher and Andrew, who make me proud to be a father everyday, and to my parents, Albert and Fannie Mae, for instilling in me a good work ethic. Sincere appreciation must be accorded to Toyota, which introduced me to the Toyota Production System, and to all of the HLS clients throughout the world for allowing me to continue to learn.

Rick Harris

Contents

Foreword

Rick Harris may be the most practical and detail-oriented person I've ever met. He paid enormous attention to the finest details of the Toyota Production System while working as a manager at the Georgetown, Kentucky, complex. And now, with his equally detail-oriented son, Chris, he is ready to share the details of developing a lean-thinking workforce in any production facility.

In this book, Rick and Chris walk you through a simple, step-by-step guide for taking a mass production workforce—consisting of production associates, team leaders, and area supervisors—and turning it into a lean production workforce with the necessary skills, training, and attitude to march in a new direction.

There is nothing fancy here. The authors simply tell you, "First you need to do this. And then you need to do this. And then you need to do this." There is nothing complicated, once Rick and Chris get through explaining it. Indeed, it seems almost too simple. "Doesn't everyone know to do this?" you may ask. Well perhaps they do, but any sample of current-day management practices in manufacturing companies, and particularly in smaller facilities, will show that if everyone knows what to do, very few act on their knowledge. This volume should help everyone get started.

Even in those facilities where considerable progress has been made, the real question remains whether or not it can be sustained. Most of us are better at planning and doing—the first two steps of the Plan/Do/Check/Act problem-solving method—than we are at the check and act steps (also called reflect and adjust at Toyota). Yet these are the keys to sustainable results. Rick and Chris's emphasis on quick response to problems by team leaders and supervisors and the auditing of every step in every process on a fixed interval is, therefore, especially useful.

Most of us are now far enough down the path in lean production to realize that the results lie in the details. This short volume presents all of the details you will need to create a frontline workforce and system of direct supervision that can effectively plan, do, reflect, and adjust, as you move your own operations steadily ahead.

Jim Womack
Chairman, Lean Enterprise Institute
Cambridge, Massachusetts
October 2006

Introduction

Why You Need This Book

In 2005, we and coauthor Earl Wilson were awarded the Shingo Prize for our book *Making Materials Flow*. During the award ceremony, we listened to numerous speakers representing facilities that were being honored at the event, and a common theme soon became apparent. That common theme was the people. Almost invariably, the individuals accepting the awards would say something like, "I could not have done it without the people" or "without the people, this would not have been possible." These and similar phrases confirmed for us that people are key in the successful implementation of lean manufacturing systems.

Changing from a mass-manufacturing environment to a lean environment is a significant process. It is a change that will ultimately affect all levels of a company. If the implementation is done correctly, the results can be outstanding. Many times, however, we have seen lean implementers become so involved with the nuts and bolts of lean implementation that the "people" side of the business is neglected. Yet, as the leaders honored at the Shingo award ceremony noted, people are critical to the change and merit attention.

This workbook has been developed to assist you in changing the way your facility looks at its people. It provides the building blocks of a Human Resources development system, but it also asks you to examine the unique characteristics of your own company. As you read, you'll be asked to consider ideas for making the most of the people in your facility.

What You'll Find in This Book

This book follows the lean journey of Rudrey Manufacturing, a company that found itself in the same position as other companies embarking on the transition to lean: learning to continually improve processes and planning to utilize employees to accomplish this task. This book outlines Rudrey's journey to developing a lean-thinking workforce.

Several chapters include exercises for the reader to work through. (Note that there are no exercises in the nitty-gritty training chapters that emphasize sharing training methods rather than brainstorming lean implementation ideas.) These exercises should help you focus on what is happening in your facility. Completing the exercises helps make your next steps clear; they provide an easily followed roadmap for implementing a comprehensive system to develop lean thinkers in your facility.

How This Book Is Organized

This book is organized to help you in three ways. First, it explains how to understand the current state of Human Resources in your facility and shows how a systematic method of training can help you develop those resources into a lean-thinking workforce. Secondly, it provides sample training sessions and explanations that you can immediately use to begin training and involving your employees.

Finally, the book identifies two major Human Resources policy practices that benefit facilities tremendously. These practices explain in some detail how to continuously train associates (whether they are newly hired or being retrained for work in new areas within the facility) and how to promote employees from within the facility to become effective team leaders and group leaders.

Chapter 1: Understanding the Role of Human Resources in a Lean Facility

Chapter 1 introduces Rudrey Manufacturing and explains where the company felt it needed to go. (You will probably see some similarities to your own company!) The chapter discusses old (pre-lean) ways of dealing with employees and contrasts those with employee relations in a lean environment. The chapter also explores the Human Resources department at Rudrey and discusses what roles the department currently has. Finally, it addresses the question of whether or not (and how) a Human Resources department can be a change agent in a facility.

Chapter 2: Preparing to Develop a Lean-Thinking Workforce

Chapter 2 is a comprehensive look at training needs for a company moving toward lean. In creating a lean environment, a company needs to develop a systematic training program that lets everyone understand what lean manufacturing means, why the company is implementing it, and how jobs are going to change.

Chapter 3: Lean 101

In this chapter, we explain why it is not enough to say, "Do it because I said so!" Managers have to take the time and effort to explain to associates and supervisors why a company is implementing lean manufacturing. They must also be adept at showing that contrary to popular belief, the implementation of lean is not about turning everyone's life upside-down but about helping a company compete successfully in a global marketplace. There are many myths concerning lean manufacturing, and successful organizations take appropriate steps to dispel them, making it easier for everyone to move forward effectively.

Chapter 4: Workplace Organization

Chapter 4 addresses several important questions (What is workplace organization? Why is it necessary? What is the 6S system? How do we do it?) and provides a simple, easily understandable, and to-the-point template of actual workplace organization training that you can use to develop your own training module.

Chapter 5: Value Stream Maps

What is a value stream map? How does it affect associates and supervisors? Why do we need it? Chapter 5 answers these questions and explains the purpose of value stream maps in a lean facility. In addition, this chapter gives you a sample training module on value stream maps.

Chapter 6: Continuous (One-Piece) Flow

In the vast majority of manufacturing facilities, most associates prefer batch production. Experience shows, however, that one-piece flow works better in most cases. Where batching is the long-honored custom, there will be resistance to changing from batch manufacturing to continuous flow; this chapter helps you work with associates to show them how the lean processes will work and how one-piece flow enables and improves the process.

Chapter 7: Lean Materials Delivery Systems

Before lean, the only time Operations talked to Materials was to address a problem. With lean, the Materials department plays a more vital role. In fact, everyone on the production floor has some responsibility for the materials delivery system, and this means everyone needs training in new roles. This chapter provides a training module that explains materials delivery routes to associates and supervisors.

Chapter 8: Creating a Flexible Workforce

A hallmark of a good lean manufacturing facility is a workforce that is cross-trained, which means that one employee is trained to perform many different tasks. Well-trained employees give a company the flexibility to react to changes in personnel (due to absence, for example), production demand, and so on. This chapter discusses a system of cross-training that can help your facility get to its desired level of flexibility.

Chapter 9: Developing Group Leaders (Supervisors)

In a lean manufacturing environment, group leaders have to be the catalyst for continuous improvement, so they need to be trained and developed with that goal in mind. This chapter provides methods to develop responsive, flexible, innovative group leaders.

Chapter 10: Continually Improving Your Workforce Through New Hires, Promotions, and Ongoing Training

In a lean environment, you rely on the associates for continuous improvement efforts. For this reason, it makes sense to keep training associates to improve their own knowledge and skills. As an organization changes, both newly hired employees and currently employed associates need to be brought and kept up to speed.

No one knows your production system better than the associates who work in your facility, and you stand to gain much from promoting team leaders and group leaders from within the organization. With a systematic approach to continually training the workforce, well-trained associates will add value to your facility. This chapter shows you how to make this happen, systematically and effectively.

Where to Begin

This workbook was written to give you step-by-step methods for developing your associates into lean thinkers. If you are new to lean, start with Chapter 1. If, however, you are familiar with lean, jump in wherever you need to. Use the Index and Table of Contents to decide where to begin.

Either way, try to complete all the exercises: They are there to help spur your thinking and help you plan. After going through this workbook, begin implementing your ideas as soon as possible, without worrying about whether the timing, ideas, and training are perfect. We find the best results in companies that get their knowledge quickly, plan quickly, begin implementation quickly, and never stop learning as they go down the lean path.

CHAPTER 1

Understanding the Role of Human Resources in a Lean Facility

"Human resources" is not necessarily a department; instead, the term refers to all the valuable employees who work in a facility. As your company heads down the lean manufacturing path, your human resources must develop into lean thinkers. Developing a workforce into a lean-thinking workforce does not have to be the job of the Human Resources (HR) department; the plant manager, lean coordinator, or another individual or group willing to assume the challenge can lead this initiative. We have found, however, that the Human Resources department tends to be best suited to lead the charge, simply because the business of HR is people. Human Resources specialists and generalists generally do a good job of supporting employees and taking care of their administrative needs, and most can adjust to this new process.

To be world class, a manufacturing facility has to be in the people-building business as well as the product-building business. Employees are the ones who take your facility to the next level by continually improving the manufacturing process. Companies implementing lean manufacturing systems have to give the associates the necessary tools to get this done.

This chapter introduces a sample company called Rudrey Manufacturing. It describes the significant improvements Rudrey made through its 2 years of lean implementation, as well as the current state of its industry and the fear of complacency that the company now faces. As this chapter shows, Rudrey began to understand that there is a lot of very valuable information on the production floor but had not yet found ways to obtain and use that information effectively. To accomplish this, Rudrey management developed a different thought process. This transition began with a series of questions that all companies moving toward lean (including yours) should address.

As the chapter progresses, it presents the questions mentioned above and descriptions of employees' roles and the role of the Human Resources department (current and future). The exercises in the chapter are designed to get you to think a little differently about the human resources in your company. The chapter ends with a description of key players in this initiative and a description and explanation of HR's internal customers.

Introducing Rudrey Manufacturing Incorporated

Throughout this workbook, we use Rudrey Manufacturing Incorporated as our primary example of a manufacturing facility going lean. Rudrey manufactures toy trucks for retail distribution. Fifteen years ago, Rudrey was profitable and had a positive outlook on its future. However, changes in the marketplace—including competitors in lower-wage regions and a higher emphasis on quality—placed Rudrey in a precarious position, and the company was less profitable than expected. Rudrey realized that it needed to make a change. After researching the best ways to change a company, Rudrey chose to go down the lean manufacturing path and adopt a plan of action based on the Toyota Production System.

Rudrey's Move to Lean Manufacturing

Rudrey has now been implementing lean manufacturing systems for approximately 2 years with great successes. The company has drawn value stream maps for all of its value streams and has made significant strides in eliminating the low-hanging fruit. It has also attacked its pacemaker[1] processes and created stability by creating continuous flow. The company's next step is to complete a timed materials delivery system throughout the facility, a process already in the early stage of implementation.

---

1. The pacemaker process is the point farthest downstream in the value stream that you can schedule to takt time and flow freely from that point forward.

Gains Rudrey Has Made Via Lean Manufacturing

As the figures below illustrate, many changes have occurred throughout the facility. Figure 1-1 shows Rudrey before the company implemented lean manufacturing, and Figure 1-2 shows Rudrey 2 years into implementation. Rudrey's accomplishments to date include the following:

- Inventory turns went from 11 to 55 in the first 2 years.
- Rudrey no longer builds to forecast but to customer pull.
- There is now only one schedule per value stream at the pacemaker. (One schedule is at the pacemaker process, with the remainder of the value stream operating with flow or pull systems.)

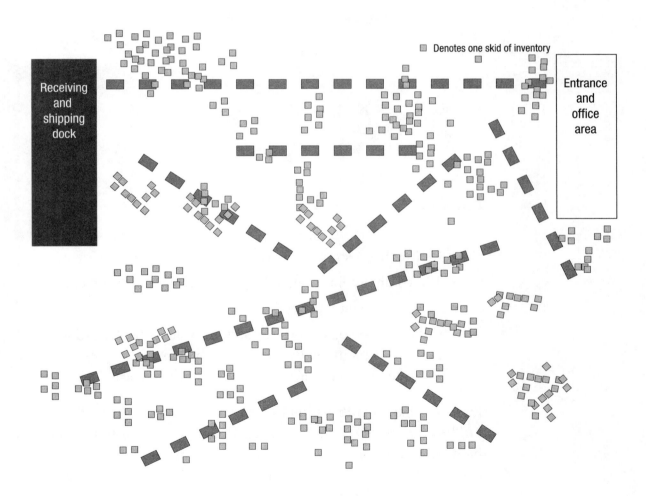

Figure 1-1.

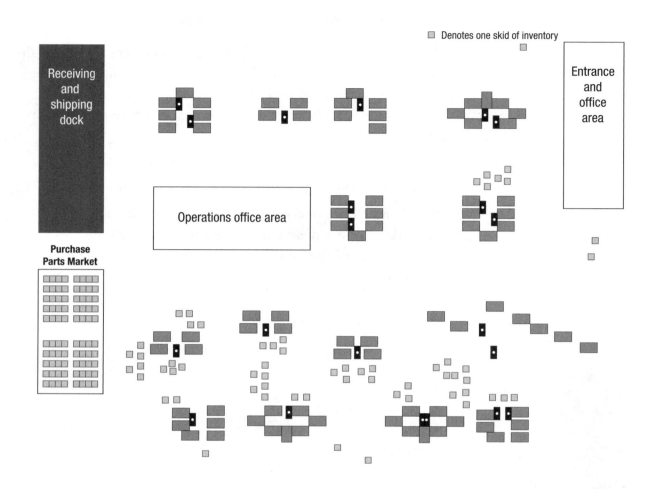

Figure 1-2.

- Rudrey has seen a 30 percent productivity improvement.
- The company has seen a 28 percent reduction in inventory.
- Scrap has been reduced by 29 percent.
- Customer responsiveness or service is at 98 percent (that is, 98 percent of the time, Rudrey can provide what a customer needs, when the customer needs it), versus 84 percent before lean.

Rudrey is happy with its improvements but knows it has other opportunities for improvement. Although Rudrey's position in the market is improving, the company is still in a very competitive environment, and company leaders worry that the facility's impressive successes may cause complacency.

Rudrey recognizes a common trap, into which many companies going down the lean journey fall. The trap is contentment, embodied in statements like, "We worked hard for 2 years, and now we can take a break," or "How do we just sustain what we have done?" In business—whether manufacturing, processing, or service—there are only two directions: A business is either growing or withering; unfortunately, there is nothing in between. Knowing this, Rudrey management also realizes that lean manufacturing is a journey to continually improve its system, not a destination to be reached. Complacency from any department or group is detrimental to success.

Continually Improving the System

Rudrey began its lean journey by adapting the Toyota Production System to its own needs and created its own production system named the Rudrey Production System (RPS).

Seeing the HR Department as a Change Agent: Going Beyond Value Stream Mapping

Rudrey was able to improve many of its processes by following value stream maps, moving machines, and implementing the RPS, but there was still potential for improvement. Like many companies that have begun the lean journey, Rudrey saw positive changes even without thoroughly training its people and getting all departments of its business involved. But the company soon discovered that opportunities existed beyond what showed up on a value stream map. Although value stream mapping the production floor is the place to start in a lean implementation, other parts of the business need to be addressed. Many companies like Rudrey have begun to look into these areas.

Rudrey looked at its Purchasing, Sales, and Design departments and attempted to implement some lean principles. At the same time, Rudrey looked at improving the Human Resources department's processes through administrative value stream mapping. Management knew that the role of the Human Resources department would have to be modified if it were to become a change agent for the facility.

Many companies do not view the Human Resources department as a change agent. However, given how much employees can impact the

---

Exercise

Can your HR department play a role in your lean production system? If so, what role?

---

bottom line, HR can influence a company more than most departments. Who, for example, is the only type of employee that, in the eyes of the customer, adds value to the product? It is the hourly production associate. Knowing this, the next question to address is "How much information does an organization give the person who adds value to the product about lean manufacturing?" Depending on the company, the answer will vary: none, very little, some, or a lot.

Exercise

How much information does your company give to the people who add value to your products? What kind of information is communicated?

While beginning its lean journey, Rudrey had not formally trained many, if any, of its hourly associates on lean manufacturing systems. Production supervisors were in the same situation. With very little training, these line and/or cell leaders were expected to run the newly implemented lean manufacturing systems. Rudrey soon realized that some of its most knowledgeable employees were not being utilized to their fullest extent. The company began to explore ways to get these valuable resources to play a significant role in continuous improvement of its facility.

Exercise

How can you begin to get your employees to play a significant role in continuous improvement of your facility?

In the past, programs were implemented, but the individuals running the programs were not trained. When implementing lean, Rudrey management realized that it was not feasible to ask the hourly associates and production supervisors to help continually improve the manufacturing system if they did not know how that system was supposed to run. Rudrey decided that it needed to institute an organized system of training its employees so that the entire workforce could play a positive role in the continuous improvement of the Rudrey Production System.

In connection with this, the RPS implementation team noted, for example, that when the hourly associates and production supervisors were called on for advice, they provided extremely useful information. This made sense because the operators and supervisors were on the floor, day in and day out, producing products. These employees held valuable information that could be used to take Rudrey to the next level of efficiency.

As a result, management and the implementation team at Rudrey began to think about a term that they could use to describe the knowledge on the floor and the people that possess that knowledge. They quickly realized, however, that there was already a name for these underutilized resources: human resources. After this discovery, Rudrey realized that it had not included the Human Resources department as much as it could have during the implementation of its new lean production system. The company had not sent any of its Human

Resources professionals to its lean training and had not approached
HR about its potential role in the lean implementation. For the
company to be truly successful, this would have to change.

Reviewing the Traditional Role of HR

Before considering Human Resources' role in a lean facility, Rudrey
thought it was important to understand HR's current role. Understanding HR's current state was a prerequisite for developing a new role for
the department.

At the time, the Human Resources department dealt with a great deal
of administrative and personal issues for the employees. For example,
the Human Resources department provided marriage, alcohol, and
credit counseling to employees as well as helping with payroll administration and other legal issues. The department was also in charge of
hiring, disciplining, and terminating employees. By performing these
functions, the Human Resources department at Rudrey had done a
good job of supporting the facility in its current state.

Exercise

What has been the role of HR in your company?

The problem with the current state was that the Operations department had not asked Human Resources to assist in the development of
lean-thinking employees. Operations, as a department, had called
upon Human Resources only when it needed something, for example,
a new employee. Human Resources hired the employee, and it was left
to Operations to train and teach this person. In short, the Human
Resources department at Rudrey had done a good job at handling the

administrative side of employee relations, but had not been asked to ensure that the new employee understood the system or the position within the system he or she had been hired to fill. Furthermore, HR had not been asked by the company to play a role in ensuring that employees become lean thinkers on the production floor.

Rudrey was aware of this current state and that it was built on the back of a traditional HR model. In the past, there was little need to train people on the floor about a particular system because there was really no system to learn. The result was that employees were utilized about 65 percent, which meant there was, on average, about 39 seconds worth of work for every 60 seconds the hourly associate was at the process. Because many of the jobs in question did not require much skill due to the underutilization, it did not really matter who was hired for a job as long as someone did it. Jobs in a lean manufacturing environment, however, are much more complex and require a greater degree of efficiency, so employees need to be much better trained.

The production floor at Rudrey has evolved over the past 30 years. Operations has gone through many different programs (commonly referred to as flavor-of-the-month programs), from trying to automate all the processes so that the employees never touched a part to trying to simplify processes so that the employees did not have to think while working. But for the RPS to be successful, management knew that the employees on the floor had to play a significant role in the continual improvement of the system. The value-added associates had to be given the knowledge and tools to be successful.

The same was true for production supervisors. They had also been through many different programs, right along with the hourly employees. Having a college degree was essentially the sole qualification needed to become a production supervisor; after starting the job, the supervisor was simply expected to perform his or her duties adequately. Supervisors received little or no training; they were responsible only for producing a lot of product.

As the information in the previous paragraphs suggests, the past mass manufacturing practices at Rudrey did not see humans as resources at all. Employees were a means to an end or an easily replaced commodity. Human Resources activities supported traditional mass manufacturing practices adequately.

Going Lean with HR

When Rudrey realized that the method of handling Human Resources in its current state would not adequately support the company's future manufacturing strategies, it also realized it needed a department that was responsible for developing employees into lean thinkers. This did not mean that the company needed a new department. It meant that Rudrey needed a Human Resources department that provides the necessary training and resources to help put knowledge possessed by production floor employees into productive and efficient practice. However, Rudrey, like many companies on their lean journeys, did not have a successful infrastructure in place to utilize this knowledge on the floor.

Information Is the Key

Rudrey management was convinced that a major asset in the lean transformation would be employees. The lean coordinator for the facility, the Operations department, and upper levels of management met with the Human Resources department to discuss the best place to begin the transformation of the Human Resources department from its current state into a change agent. To accomplish this transformation, the team looked at what they thought was missing most. They came to the conclusion that a huge information gap existed and that most people in the facility could not answer the most basic questions about what was happening (e.g., "What is lean?" or "Am I going to lose my job?" or "Why are we doing this?"). The group came to a consensus that it needed to determine what information was needed and how it would begin to get this information to the people who needed it. The Rudrey team addressed the following questions:

- What is the necessary information?
- Do the associates have the necessary information?
- What is the role of the hourly associate in the implementation of the RPS?
- Do associates know what to do within the RPS?
- Do associates understand their role in the continuous improvement of the RPS?
- Do associates know how to make an improvement to the RPS?

- Are expectations communicated clearly?
- Do associates know what to do if they have a quality problem?
- Do associates understand the importance of a pull system and other aspects of lean manufacturing?
- Does everyone understand why material needs to move quickly?
- Does everyone know where they need to be and when?
- Are there guides to let associates know where they need to be next?
- Does management know who can do what job?
- Does management know what output can be expected when an associate is added or subtracted?
- Does management have a lean plan for newly hired employees?
- Does management have a lean plan for future promotions?

The preceding questions are not all encompassing, but they give a good starting point. Use them to assess what is happening in your own organizations.

Obviously, a lot of information needs to be conveyed to the workforce, but relaying this information had not been a priority for Rudrey; the company simply did not see the value in having good information flow.

The Triangle of Involvement

Information has always provided a sense of importance in Rudrey's facility (i.e., "If I am the only person who has this information, I am important to the company"), but the *flow* of information was limited. Eventually, Rudrey began to realize that because the company operated in a culture of information withholding, it was not getting valuable input from the workforce. Rudrey decided that it would be the responsibility of Human Resources department to tackle the difficult task of creating information flow. The first step was to develop a triangle of involvement. See Figure 1-3. The corners of this triangle are Human Resources, Operations, and a Lean Coordinator.

- **Lean Coordinator:** At Rudrey, the Lean Coordinator's role is to ensure that any decisions made about the workforce fit correctly

Exercises

What is the necessary information?

Do the associates have the necessary information?

What is the role of the hourly associate in the implementation of the lean production system?

Do associates know what to do within the lean production system?

Do associates understand their role in the continuous improvement of the lean production system?

Do associates know how to make an improvement to the lean production system?

Are expectations communicated clearly?

Do associates know what to do if they have a quality problem?

Do associates understand the importance of a pull system and other aspects of lean manufacturing?

Does everyone understand why material needs to move quickly?

Does everyone know where they need to be, and when?

Are there guides to let associates know where they need to be next?

Does management know who can do what job?

Does management know what output can be expected when an associate is added or subtracted?

Does management have a lean plan for newly hired employees?

Does management have a lean plan for future promotions?

into the Rudrey Production System. Therefore, this person must be involved with any decisions concerning the workforce.

- **Operations:** Another corner of the triangle is Operations. It is important for any facility to realize that the associates on the floor are the ones adding value to the product. Decisions concerning them must include Operations because Rudrey cannot disrupt the flow of manufacturing.

- **Human Resources:** The Human Resources department understands that money is made on the floor (by adding value to the product) and that it needs to be in constant contact with the Lean Coordinator and Operations to ensure decisions concerning the workforce are beneficial for both the operating system and the employees. For the facility to be profitable, Operations needs to run efficiently and any decisions made by Human Resources should be made with that in mind.

Triangle of the Human Resources Department Involvement

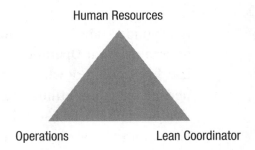

Figure 1-3.

Identifying HR's Customer(s)

Rudrey has learned throughout its lean implementation that it is important to identify the customer and find out what each one requires. The Human Resources department is no different; HR discovered that its customer is Operations (or, more specifically, the Rudrey Production System). This was a novel concept and may have been uncomfortable for Human Resources (just as it was uncomfortable for Materials and Maintenance to realize that Operations was their customer). Like any change, moving to a lean environment causes some discomfort. It is important to remember that this feeling usually subsides once people see the benefits of change. One immediate benefit is the ease with which decisions can be made once everyone is able to see a clearly defined customer. This is a hallmark of lean manufacturing and works equally well for other processes. In fact, running a facility with internal customers in mind is a necessity for a successful lean transformation.

Exercise

Who is/are the customer(s) of your Human Resources department?

After understanding that there was a customer to support, HR had to determine what Operations required from the HR department. Rudrey had been going down the lean path long enough to realize what it needed was to continually improve its system, so the answer was relatively simple: A lean-thinking, flexible workforce, along with experienced and knowledgeable leaders prepared to help in the continuous improvement efforts of the facility.

Exercise

What do your customers require from your Human Resources department? That is, what are your customers' needs?

This answer is what drove the Human Resources department at Rudrey to develop a comprehensive Human Resources system to support lean manufacturing, while also developing the necessary environment to foster a culture of continuous improvement. The decisions to be made by Human Resources revolve around the following mission statement:

The Human Resources department at Rudrey Manufacturing Incorporated exists to develop a lean-thinking, flexible workforce, along with experienced, knowledgeable leaders that are prepared to help in the continuous improvement efforts of the facility.

Exercise

Develop your own HR mission statement.

Summing Up

- Understand the past practices of the HR department.

- Realize the potential of an HR department that plays the role of change agent.

- Recognize the need for HR to be in constant contact with Operations and the lean coordinator.

- Define the customer(s) and the customer's needs.

- Define a mission statement for HR.

CHAPTER 2

Preparing to Develop a Lean-Thinking Workforce

A company's Human Resources department can play the role of change agent. It can change the way that the workforce views lean manufacturing and how employees operate in a lean manufacturing system.

The Human Resources department (HRD) at Rudrey, now with a specific mission (see Chapter 1), had to develop a strategy. They approached this by determining the following criteria, covered in more depth throughout the rest of this chapter:

- **Who needs to be trained:** With different classifications of employees, you must first determine who needs the training. Supervisors? Line associates? Maintenance staff? With limited resources, most HR departments cannot train everyone at the same time and must prioritize.

- **When the training should take place:** There is an optimal time to train employees on the subject matter. The best time to provide training is a few days before implementation, so that the operators will be prepared. It is important to find out whether this timing is possible.

- **What information will be covered in the training:** Once HR assumes responsibility for training all of the company's employees, it must develop training material and determine what information to cover, ensuring that the employees have the tools they need to improve the process.

- **Where the training will be held:** Some training may be held offsite, and some onsite. Location depends on which venue is best for a company's training program.

- **How the training will be administered:** For example, how long will the training be? The length of training time should be appropriate for the material being presented. Human Resources must also determine training format (e.g., workshop, lecture, or roundtable).

By addressing these issues, the Human Resources department can effectively develop a strategy to train a lean-thinking workforce. Although this strategy may not be complete and will continually change and improve, it will provide the department with a foundation for the training program.

Determining Who Needs to Be Trained—and How Soon

For Rudrey, the short answer to the question of whom to train was "everyone." However, that answer alone does not get Rudrey any closer to developing a lean-thinking workforce. Because value-added hourly associates and production supervisors are the employees most immediately affected, many companies make best use of their resources to train those employees first. These employees are charged with running and continually improving the system, and they need to have the knowledge to accomplish this task successfully. Thoroughly training these employees means you have prepared employees to continually improve the production process; that ability is likely to be the organization's sustainable competitive advantage for years to come.

Establishing a Training Hierarchy

The problem Rudrey faced with training all of its associates and supervisors was that some areas of its facility were farther along with their lean manufacturing initiatives than others: Some parts of manufacturing had been going down the lean path for 2 years, some 1 year, and some had not yet been touched by the implementation. This meant that the company could not progress its employees down the path of lean training at the same time or in the same way. Rudrey worked with Operations and the lean coordinator to identify the areas of the facility at the highest level of implementation, meaning the ones that had gone the farthest down the lean path. The training hierarchy established at this time was tailored to accommodate these differences.

- **High priority; train immediately:** In a lean transformation, certain parts of the facility are more "lean" than others at any given time. At Rudrey, these were areas that had implemented workplace organization, posted value stream maps, moved into manufacturing cells, and were beginning their material movement initiatives.

- **Training needed:** Rudrey then worked to identify which areas had implemented *some* lean initiatives. These areas had also implemented workplace organization, posted value stream maps, and moved into the cellular manufacturing concept, but they had yet to begin their material movement initiatives.

- **Plan training:** Some areas had not done much at all in terms of lean implementation. They had heard about lean and about lean manufacturing, but lean had not yet changed their jobs.

Exercise

Keeping these three groupings in mind, how do the employees in your facility fit into each?

_____   _____   _____
_____   _____   _____
_____   _____   _____
_____   _____   _____
_____   _____   _____
_____   _____   _____
_____   _____   _____
_____   _____   _____

Determining the Optimal Timing

Rudrey determined it had to begin with those areas farther down the road, those identified as "high priority; train immediately." The team decided to train those employees right away, and the following courses were created: Lean 101, workplace organization, value stream maps, continuous flow, and materials delivery routes. Because a goal of training is that employees be prepared to assist in the implementation process and continually improve the process after implementation, the ideal timing for training employees on each subject is a couple of days before implementation. For example, if a continuous flow manufacturing cell is to be implemented on a Wednesday, you want to train the affected associates on that Monday. This is the optimal time, giving employees a day to ask questions and process the information. At Rudrey, some "high priority; train immediately" areas had already been exposed to lean concepts or lean strategies; the thrust in these areas was training that reinforced what was being applied correctly and training that corrected misconceptions or filled in knowledge gaps.

Retaining Information

In agreement with Operations and the lean coordinator, the Rudrey's HR department also determined that it would be best to train the rest of the facility after it trained the high-priority group. In the second group (Training needed), however, after advancing employees to an acceptable level on concepts already implemented, HR began training them in new areas, just before implementing those new lean concepts. Rudrey saw it as beneficial if the initial training sessions were held in classrooms with the employees then practicing what they had learned on the shop floor in the next couple of days. Knowing that new ideas are retained best if they are applied quickly, Rudrey planned their training carefully. For example, it would not be beneficial to train operators on materials delivery 2 months before the materials delivery system was implemented. When training occurs this far before employees can use the information, much of the information is lost. Because Rudrey's HR department wanted future training to be effective, they worked closely with Operations and the Lean Coordinator to determine dates of implementation and, thus, training schedules.

Developing Training Materials

The Rudrey training team (Operations, the Lean Coordinator, and Human Resources) also needed to develop training materials. Rudrey decided that the Lean Coordinator would assume the primary responsibility of developing these materials, but quickly realized that this individual would need a lot of help collecting and organizing the necessary information. To facilitate this process, management created a team that included a representative from Operations, a representative from the Human Resources department, a representative from the Materials department, and a representative from Maintenance.

Exercise

What groups should be represented on your training-development team?

A training-development team is *not* the arena to try to sway someone toward the lean way of thinking. This is the arena for lean-thinking people to gather and constructively assemble training materials that will improve their facility. Rudrey realized that this team was going to be critical to the success of the program so it chose employees already on board with the change to lean manufacturing.

Each person on the new team had a particular perspective and was knowledgeable in his or her area. For example, the Materials department was knowledgeable on material flow. The Lean Coordinator, through reading and implementing, also knew how the materials should flow in a lean facility. Together, they developed a solid training session on what information they wanted to provide in the materials delivery system training. The other individuals on the team served as critics to ascertain that the information was hitting the mark.

Through this process (and also by following the processes outlined in reference materials used throughout previous lean implementation), the team was successful in getting the necessary material together.

Lean 101 (described in the following section) was the same for all areas, but Rudrey customized the remaining sessions, tailoring them to specific groups being trained.

Exercise

Keeping in mind that all of your employees will eventually be trained, and that the training material will be developed for first-line manufacturing employees, which groups will likely require customization of the training materials?

One of the lessons the Rudrey team learned while creating training materials was that not all materials work well with all employees. When developing material for administrative areas such as purchasing, sales, quality, and so on, the team found it was sensible *not* to use manufacturing examples. This proved, in fact, a wise decision. Administrative areas do not want to hear about how lean manufacturing happens on the floor as much as they want to know how it is going to happen in their offices and cubicles. The best approach is to remove all manufacturing examples in the training materials and replace them with administrative examples.

Exercise

What non-manufacturing examples can you think of to use when training administrative personnel?

Rudrey also realized that employees learn in different ways: some by doing (individual or group exercises), some by seeing (visual examples, handouts, and so on), some by hearing (lecture), and some with a combination of these three approaches. The team members took great pains to design courses so that all three ways of learning were tapped. They put together simple PowerPoint presentations that included in-class participation exercises.

Exercise

Think about how you learn best. Do you enjoy listening to an hour-long lecture? Do you appreciate handouts on which to make notes? Do you learn from exercises that illustrate the points being discussed? Do you like seeing visual aids that add to the material being presented? Make notes of all your preferences, and ask your colleagues for theirs.

The courses were not designed to make every employee a lean guru. They were structured to give specific information about lean that employees could use in their everyday jobs. Therefore, each one-hour workshop had a specific goal. By outlining specific goals for each course, the trainers let the people being trained understand what was expected during each session. They followed age-old training wisdom: Indicate what is going to be taught (that is, state the goal), teach it, and sum it up to ensure that the goal was met.

Finally, at the end of each training course, the training-development team handed out a feedback and evaluation form so that the participants could help continually improve the training modules by letting the team know whether or not the training goal(s) had been met for each session. These forms included sections for open-ended questions and scaled questions (see Figure 2-1). The training-development team met after each session to discuss the feedback and determine how to improve the modules. The high priority areas were a great resource for these forms because employees in these areas had already implemented many of the principles and were able to provide exceptionally valuable feedback to the training staff.

Training module: _____

Instructor: _____

Date: _____

Group: _____

	Poor					Excellent	
How would you rate the information?	1	2	3	4	5	6	7
How would you rate the method of presentation?	1	2	3	4	5	6	7
How would you rate the training room?	1	2	3	4	5	6	7
How would you rate the handouts?	1	2	3	4	5	6	7
How would you rate the instructor?	1	2	3	4	5	6	7

Were the goals of the session clearly communicated, and do you feel that they were covered sufficiently? (Please explain.)

_____

_____

_____

Do you think that the goals of this training module are important to the implementation of lean manufacturing in your area? (Please explain.)

_____

_____

_____

What was not covered in this module that you think would be beneficial? Why would this be useful?

_____

_____

_____

Do you feel that this module has helped your ability to continually improve the manufacturing process? (Please explain.)

_____

_____

_____

What would you do to improve this training module?

_____

_____

_____

Figure 2-1.

Lean 101

Lean 101 makes a case for implementing lean manufacturing, addresses what employees may have heard, discusses lean manufacturing myths and what lean is really about, and attempts to address some of the employees' apprehension. Lean 101 also includes a description of the seven forms of waste.

Workplace Organization

Rudrey knew that having a well-organized facility is the bedrock of an effective lean manufacturing system, so the company's workplace organization module utilized the 6S process, derived from Toyota's 5S approach. (The final S, safety, was added by those implementing lean production systems.) This course took participants through a step-by-step approach to implementing workplace organization.

Value Stream Maps

Value stream mapping training was based on understanding what is on the value stream map, not on *drawing* one. Because the value stream map is a central tool for lean implementation, Rudrey wanted the participants to be able to recognize the maps, read them, and understand them.

Continuous Flow

Continuous flow training addressed the concept of one-piece flow and how operators would be affected by the change. An explanation of standardized work was also included in Rudrey's continuous flow course—it is an important part of a lean manufacturing system, and Rudrey wanted to convey this message to its workforce. This course also answered some of the questions related to how the frontline supervisors' jobs would begin to change.

Materials Delivery System

Materials delivery system training outlined why the materials need to move quickly. In addition, it addressed the responsibilities of the hourly associate and the value-added operator, who plays a simple though significant role in the materials delivery system of the Rudrey facility.

Additional Training

Rudrey did not stop with these five courses. While utilizing these five training modules as the basis for the training program, the company constantly sought new ideas for training. When a new idea for training emerged, the training-development team reconvened to discuss it. If the group believed the additional training would add value to the organization, they proceeded to develop a course. Before offering this course, however, they made sure that the initial five-course base was still solid and was accomplishing what it was intended to do.

Knowing Where, How Long, and By Whom the Workforce Needs to Be Trained

Deciding Where to Train

Where to train was easily decided by Rudrey: The training was to occur in the lean room. This room at the Rudrey facility is where lean manufacturing meetings are held. On the walls are slogans and quick reference sheets to terminology, plus all the current and future value stream maps and the implementation plans for the facility. Because the room is in-house, participants had easy access.

Exercise

Think of locations for training, including various onsite rooms and offsite locations. After creating a list, write down the pros and cons of each.

Knowing How Long Training Sessions Should Last

At first, this question seemed insignificant to the Rudrey HR department, Operations department, and the Lean Coordinator, but as they discussed the matter, they realized they also needed to investigate the answer. After interviewing individuals who regularly taught lean manufacturing workshops, they concluded that workshop participants could realistically comprehend and digest about an hour of material at a time. After an hour, a break of some sort was essential.

The Rudrey team talked more with everyone involved and decided to train in one-hour blocks (instead of training for longer periods, with frequent breaks). This provided some positive outcomes for the facility in general. The first was that a one-hour block of time did not tie up employees, something that would have made it harder on Operations to run the facility. Obviously, it was easier for Operations and Materials to plan for their employees to be gone approximately an hour than to shut down for an entire day. The one-hour block also meant that the Lean Coordinator would not spend an entire day training and that the plant management could attend the short sessions without disrupting their schedules. In short, by scheduling training in one-hour blocks, Rudrey was able to be quite flexible, both in designing the training module and in scheduling frequency.

It was not enough, however, to plan the day and set up a session. The team also had to plan the hour. They kicked around the idea of having a paid lunch meeting, but the training team did not really like that idea, because they were afraid that eating would be a distraction. They considered the end of the day, but that idea was abandoned because the end of the day was normally pretty hectic and everyone's attention is focused on problems accumulated during the day or on going home. The team then considered the beginning of the day, but this raised concerns about startup issues. They finally decided to hold training after the first facility-wide break. This would allow for a solid start up, and the plant management agreed to set aside this block of time and attend the training sessions. Note that what worked for Rudrey is not set in stone. Another time may work better for your facility, but weigh the pros and cons of every timeframe considered before deciding what is most suitable.

Exercise

When can you schedule one-hour sessions at your facility? Keep in mind both non-manufacturing attendees and second- and third-shift workers.

Designating Who Should Conduct the Training and Who Should Be Trained

"Who needs to train the associates?" was a question Rudrey often thought about. At first, the company considered using the supervisor of those being trained, but the training-development team quickly abandoned that idea because the supervisors themselves were not yet well trained in lean. Another option was to go outside the organization and hire a professional trainer or consultant. That idea was also quickly abandoned; Rudrey wanted the RPS to be developed by Rudrey personnel, not outsiders. Finally, Rudrey selected the Lean Coordinator, who was proficient in lean manufacturing and had already assumed the task of developing the training materials, with the help of the training team. The plant manager was Rudrey's lean champion, but the Lean Coordinator would be the face of the transformation on the production floor because she would be the one training employees in the facility. Understanding this responsibility, the lean coordinator wanted to improve her training skills, as every trainer should, so she was periodically sent offsite to attend lean manufacturing workshops, gain more knowledge, and sharpen her skills.

The next question was, "Who needs to be present at the training?" Rudrey realized that it did not make a lot of sense to have a Lean 101 workshop about how management was going to work with the workforce to create an efficient manufacturing system if top management ignored the workshop. In total agreement with this, Rudrey management determined that the plant manager would kick off every training session with a few comments. One anecdotal example demonstrates how much Rudrey supported this idea. When the plant manager was sick and could not attend one of the earliest of the scheduled training sessions, the company cancelled the session until the manager recovered and could attend.

The company also decided that the supervisor of the area and a Human Resources representative should also be present at every training session. A Human Resources representative needed to be there because HR's role was changing. Once focused more on administrative functions, the department was now helping to develop and improve the company's most valuable asset: its people. Supervisors needed to attend the sessions to learn about lean and to grasp exactly what their employees were learning.

Creating a Lean Training Path

Knowing which courses to teach is not enough; HR also needs to know in which order to teach them. To this end, the Rudrey training team developed a lean training path (LTP): the path employees in the facility would go through and the order of progression. See Figure 2-2. It became the responsibility of the Human Resources department to get all employees, both hourly and salary, successfully through the LTP.

Figure 2-2.

Rudrey management, HR, Operations, and the Lean Coordinator, worked in tandem to develop a path with a logical progression. All of those involved in this process felt strongly that Lean 101 should be the first training session to introduce all employees (hourly, salary, purchasing, sales, etc.) to lean, systematically and consistently.

The second training step on the path was workplace organization (6S). Rudrey decided that it wanted to train employees on workplace organization before that stage of lean manufacturing was implemented. Recognizing that Rudrey associates had a lot to offer in the implementation of workplace organization, the training team also decided that the company's continuous improvement team should spend time in the work areas where employees had just been trained, to conduct *kaizen* events.[1] This ensured that the structured training sessions were supplemented by hands-on training in a continuous improvement event.

After an area implemented its workplace organization principles, employees would progress to value stream maps. Value stream map training is not, as a rule, urgent until the maps are drawn, because the hourly associates and production supervisors are usually not the ones who draw the maps. In Rudrey's case, industrial engineers and management drew the maps on most occasions. But although the hourly associates and supervisors did not need to know how to draw a value stream map, it was important for all employees in the facility to understand what a value stream is, what it says, and how to use the value stream map.

The next training session focused on continuous flow. Ideally, this training is scheduled 2 days before the implementation of the continuous flow principles on the floor, thus preparing operators to understand and assist in the changes that will be made in their areas.

Lean materials delivery systems was the next training session because it was important for employees to understand their role in the materials delivery system. That role, although minimal, is vital to the success of the materials delivery system. In the past, many Rudrey hourly Operations associates felt they had no responsibility for Materials

---

1. A *kaizen* event is a continuous improvement event in which an individual or group concentrates on improving a certain area for a set period of time.

because Materials was a distinct department. In the Rudrey manufacturing system however, Operations had a role, and that role was important. This training was scheduled 2 days before the lean materials delivery principles were to be implemented.

Although lean materials delivery systems was the last scheduled training session, Rudrey knew that there would be more at a later date, and those would be scheduled as needed.

Summing Up

- Determine who needs to be trained.
- Determine when they need to be trained.
- Determine what information needs to be covered in the training.
- Determine a good place to hold the training.
- Determine how the material will be presented to the attendees (length, the trainer, the method, etc.).

CHAPTER 3

Lean 101

Lean 101 is a beginner's introduction to lean but serves equally well as a refresher course or as a vehicle to clarify any misconceptions. Rudrey decided on three major goals for participants in its Lean 101 training module:

- To understand what lean manufacturing is, and what it is not
- To understand why lean manufacturing is being implemented
- To understand and recognize the seven forms of waste

What Lean Is . . . and Isn't

Some associates will probably have some preconceived ideas about lean in your facility. In the Rudrey facility, as in many organizations in the first year or two of their lean implementation, opinions about lean were negative. The word "lean" itself seemed to have a negative connotation, and poor information flow within the company further contributed to perceptions that lean would cause more problems than it was worth. Management was partly to blame for this by not telling people the whys, whats, and hows of lean. Moreover, employees looked back at other major programs that had been implemented prior to lean, programs that often led to confusion, discouragement, and most importantly, layoffs.

Rudrey decided that Lean 101 was the perfect antidote to employee skepticism. The training module would give associates good information, dispel lean myths, and describe a systematic approach to improvement.

Addressing Lean Myths

The first lean myth to be dispelled was that implementing lean results in massive layoffs. On the contrary, Rudrey had made a commitment that it would not lay anyone off due to its lean initiatives. This was a common sense commitment because layoffs do not get organizations any closer to a lean state and certainly do not promote an environment for a workforce to thrive. To defuse apprehension and resistance, Rudrey management wanted to make it clear that the company was not implementing lean systems to decrease business but to increase business and that lean would help Rudrey grow and become a major force in the global market. To grow its business, Rudrey had to have lean-thinking and flexible associates, and it was impossible for the company to meet that goal by laying off people.

Rudrey wanted to be sure that every associate was clear on this issue, because people afraid of losing their jobs would be much less likely to help in improvement efforts. To drive this point home, Rudrey used Figure 3-1 as the first slide of the training.

What Lean Manufacturing *Is Not*

- Laying off employees
- Improvements that can't be maintained
- Improving your current system

Figure 3-1.

As the figure illustrates, another lean myth is that implementing lean systems is about improving the current system. Lean 101 emphasized that lean systems do not focus on improving current systems but on changing the way a business is run. Implementing lean manufacturing is about implementing productive and efficient systems, not just a lot of random improvement tools. To stress this point, the Lean 101 trainer used an illustration on which numbers from 1 through 60 were randomly arranged (see Figure 3-2). The trainer gave session participants 60 seconds to touch all 60 numbers in numerical order. Of course, nobody got all 60 numbers; most people got between 15 and 30. When they did the exercise a second time, some people did even worse. Two important points were made: 1) Most people believe repetition is the key to getting better, but repeating the exercise did not improve results. 2) If there is no *system* to getting better, things will not get better. The outcome will be chaos.

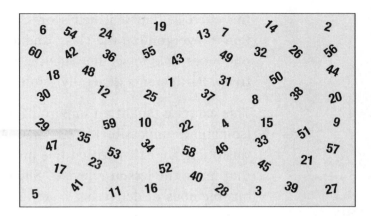

Figure 3-2.

Using a similar illustration (see Figure 3-3), the Rudrey trainer shows the class participants what would happen if the exercise were performed with a system in place. The trainer identified the two people in the class who had scored lowest in the first exercise, wrote their scores on the class white board, and boasted that scores could be doubled by giving these workers a system. The trainer then took the two participants aside and explained the system to them.

As Figure 3-3 illustrates, the system was simple but effective. The random numbers are now divided into six sections. The number 1 is in the top middle section with number 2 being in the section to the right. The remaining numbers continue to flow sequentially through the sections in a clockwise manner. (To illustrate the flow, the first twelve numbers are circled in Figure 3-3) The system made finding the numbers more efficient, and the two people who participated in

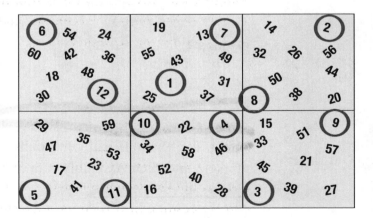

Figure 3-3.

this exercise doubled their scores. The trainer then explained the system to everyone in the class, and asked everyone to do the exercise one more time to see how having a system in place improves productivity. Participants generally doubled their scores or came very close.

This exercise taught an important lesson: Improvements are difficult (sometimes impossible) if there are no standards to improve upon. At this point, the trainer used this point to illustrate a business concept that made the lesson relevant. She did this by explaining that previous methods of delivering materials had been disorganized and inefficient and that a lean system was much more efficient. As Figure 3-4 shows, in a traditional plant layout, there is no organized way to move material. Flow is random (much like the random numbers that participants had been asked to touch in sequential order) and chaotic. The trainer then explained a lean system for moving material and information more efficiently.

Traditional Plant Layout

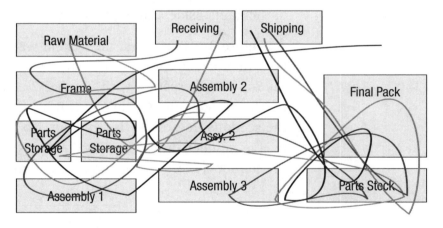

Figure 3-4.

In a lean system (see Figure 3-5), material is pulled through the system so that nothing is ever produced that does not need to be produced. For example, shipping pulls products out of Assembly 3's market,[1] and then Assembly 3 needs to replenish the market. To do

---

1. A market is a controlled level of inventory with a specific location for each item. It is handled much differently than normal stock or inventory between processes.

that, Assembly 3 must pull from Assembly 2's market. The same process goes all the way back to receiving. This is a system similar to the one Rudrey was planning to implement. The point of this explanation was to get people thinking a little differently about lean and the observable differences a lean system could make.

Future

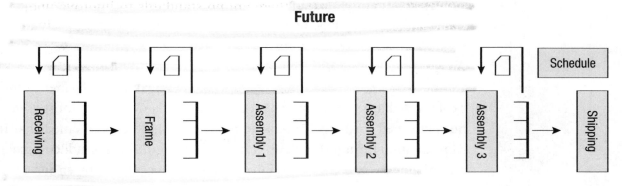

Figure 3-5.

Why Lean Is Necessary

Rudrey management realized that, in the first day of training, it was important to show associates why the plant had to change the way it did business—in other words, why it had to go to lean to survive, grow, and compete. The explanation had to be simple and honest, so the trainer discussed Rudrey's top three competitors, Rudrey's market share, and Rudrey's profitability.

This was the first time that many of the associates (as well as supervisors, management, and professional staff) had thought about competition and the first time they realized that other companies vied for the same business that Rudrey was trying to get. Moreover, the lecture and the trainer's slides showed that the competition had been succeeding; Rudrey was falling behind while its competitors were gaining market share.

- In 1990, Rudrey's market share was 29 percent.
- In 1995, Rudrey's market share was 27 percent.
- In 2000, Rudrey's market share was 25 percent.
- In 2005, Rudrey's market share was 23 percent.

Ten years earlier, Rudrey was very profitable, but that profitability had steadily declined. Although Rudrey was still profitable, future profits were questionable. Clearly, Rudrey had to do something to reverse this decline, and the change agent the company chose was lean manufacturing.

After the presentation, the trainer asked participants, "Who makes the money for the organization?" The correct answer to this question is value-added associates, because they add value to the product in the eyes of the customer, but many of the associates in the training room did not understand this concept, with good reason. In the past, they had not been treated as the organization's moneymakers. The trainer bluntly explained that the company's previous methods of manufacturing were not patterned for the value-added associate. She then explained that in lean manufacturing, the focus is on optimizing the value-added associate. Although the associates' jobs would not necessarily be easier, they would be ergonomically correct, featuring workstations designed with the value-added associate at the center of the process.

Exercise

Who are your three biggest competitors and what are they doing to try to take customers away from your businesses?

What is your market share now and what was it 5, 10, or 15 years ago?

How profitable is your organization?

The Seven Forms of Waste[2]

To make a first significant step toward a facility-wide culture of continuous improvement, Rudrey management decided to train value-added associates in the seven forms of waste, derived from the Toyota Production System. The trainer began by explaining to the associates that all seven forms of waste were a symptom. This means that the *waste* is not

---

2. The seven forms of waste are taken from Taichi Ohno's *Toyota Production System Beyond Large-Scale Production*. Portland, OR: Productivity Press, 1998. pp. 19–20.

actually the problem, but the *process that is causing the waste* is the real problem. Identifying waste is a way to determine that there is a problem and to identify that problem so that it can be fixed.

The trainer made sure that the associates knew that Rudrey was utilizing knowledge about the seven forms of waste to improve its processes, not to catch people doing something wrong. By explaining the seven forms of waste to the associates, Rudrey was preparing them to help in the implementation process. This was a logical decision for the company to make: Because associates are on the floor day in and day out, they have a good opportunity to see and identify waste.

Waste of Overproduction

Overproduction takes two forms:

- Producing more than is required by customers
- Producing products faster than customers are buying them

The waste of overproduction was difficult for the Rudrey trainers to tackle because it went directly against years of corporate culture. In the past, Rudrey management had always said "more and faster," supporting a philosophy that was all about more product, more product, and still more product. On occasion, quality suffered because the emphasis on "more product" was greater than the emphasis on "right product." This mindset worked reasonably well when Rudrey ran a very small amount of part numbers, but Rudrey, like many other companies, had begun to make a lot of different part numbers. As a result, overproduction resulted in significant cost to the organization and Rudrey had to change its philosophy as well as its system. The company would now focus on making the right parts and on making part numbers in the order and quantities that they needed to be made. The cost of overproduction was simply too high to ignore and Rudrey knew that its associates had to see overproduction in a new light: as a profit-eating activity.

Overproduction, in fact, may be the most significant form of waste, because it provides opportunities for all other forms of waste to occur. Take rework, for example. If a problem in the production process produced a defect, overproducing the product would just produce more defective product, which would require more rework. For this reason alone, it is important for Operations to produce only what is supposed to be produced, when it is supposed to be produced.

Rudrey saw discussions on the subject of overproduction as a perfect opportunity to introduce the idea of takt time,[3] the measure of how often customers bought a part from Rudrey. For example, if takt time was 30 seconds, a customer was buying a part every 30 seconds. It did not make sense for Rudrey to produce products any faster than takt time. Rudrey could not sell parts any faster, so there was no need to produce (overproduce) them any faster.

Waste of Time on Hand (Waiting)

When a system is not set up well, employees often have to wait for a machine or another associate to finish a process. When an employee is waiting, he or she is adding no value to the product. The Rudrey trainer began to address this subject with a question: "Whose fault is it that an associate is waiting during a process?" The answer is that, the majority of the time, the fault lies with management or with whoever designed the system. Waiting occurs when the system is not operating properly or is poorly designed.

Waiting is usually easy to see, but is sometimes a difficult problem to fix. You cannot just go up to an associate and say "stop waiting!" There is a reason the associate is waiting—some sort of backup at the workstations, broken (or nearly broken) machines, lack of parts, and so on. The problem is likely in the system, so it is the system (not the associate) that needs to be fixed.

Waste in Transportation (Inefficient Transportation of Material)

Inefficient transportation of material is the next form of waste the trainer discussed, and she asked the value-added associates the following questions:

- How often do you have to move material multiple times?
- How many times have you run out of parts?

3. Takt time is calculated by taking the available production time per day divided by customer demand per day. See C. Marchwinski and J. Shook, eds. *Lean Lexicon*. Brookline, MA: Lean Enterprise Institute, 2003, pp. 80.

- How many times have you not had the parts you need to complete an order?

These questions all addressed real problems Rudrey associates had faced in the past because Rudrey had never had an efficient materials delivery system that supported the value-added associates. The associates had simply been expected to do their best with what they had. The trainer then explained that the problems they had faced were significant problems because they caused productivity and profitability to decline.

At this point in the Rudrey training, the idea that movement of material can be wasteful was introduced, but not discussed in detail. The thrust of the training was to have associates understand that moving material adds no value to a product, so every time material or parts are moved, the process must be quick and efficient. A detailed discussion of materials delivery, one of Rudrey's core courses, is the subject of Chapter 7.

Waste of Processing

The trainer defined processing as doing something for customers that they are not paying you to do. For example, suppose a customer specifies that a machine weld is acceptable, but the hourly associate does not like the way it looks, so he picks up a file and files the weld down to make it look a little better. Is that waste? You bet. It is well intended, but it is wasteful, because the customer is not paying more for that extra filing down. It is not adding value to the product.

This can be a difficult point to make because many people believe that waste occurs because of bad intentions and that actions prompted by good intentions are not waste.

Processing waste may also occur because the process has simply "always been done that way." For example, if you ask Frank why he turns the part over and sands the bottom, his answer may be that Geno told him to do it that way. If you then ask Geno why he told Frank to do it that way, he may say that Andrew trained him to do it that way, and Andrew may tell you that he learned "that way" from Dale, who left the company 20 years ago. This example shows that processing waste can be difficult to track down and difficult to gauge.

There may be a good reason that the bottom of the product is sanded, but there is a lack of process control: No one knows why it is done or whether or not it really needs to be done. The reason (good, bad, or indifferent) has been lost in the past, and investigating the reason can easily take a lot of time.

Waste of Stock on Hand (Inventory)

In the past, inventory at Rudrey was always seen as a good thing, like having money in the bank or food in the cupboard. If something went wrong, if something broke, if someone did not show up, or if Operations had a really bad day, there was something to fall back on, and the facility would still be fine. As the trainer explained, however, uncontrolled inventory in a lean manufacturing environment is a bad thing, because it signals waste in the system and is very costly.

In a production environment, when you see uncontrolled, excessive inventory in the system, it is the same as seeing money lying on the floor: The facility has already paid for the raw materials and the labor hours to produce the product. The only way the facility can make money is to sell the product; instead, it is sitting on the shop floor, taking up floor space, having to be moved, or having to be reworked.

Because inventory is costly, an organization needs to take steps to reduce it. When value-added associates see inventory levels decreasing, they do not need to worry. They are seeing a change that makes the process better and the facility more profitable.

Waste of Movement (Inefficient Machine and Operator Motion)

Inefficient machine and operator motion was the next form of waste that the trainer discussed. A waste of motion is any motion by a machine or associate that does not add value to a product. If the stroke of a machine is set at 18 inches, but only 2 inches are required, waste occurs at every stroke. Associate waste may include pushing reset buttons, walking long distances to retrieve parts, reaching extra-long distances for a part, handling parts twice, and so on. In the past, these inefficient motions were not a priority concern because it was much easier to live with them than to find and fix the root cause. But in a lean environment with an efficient system, inefficient motions have to be addressed, and value-added associates, as well as management, need to recognize and resolve them.

In connection with this, the trainer asked the value-added associates, "In your process, can you think of a motion you make or a machine makes that is not necessary?" Rudrey management now operates with the understanding that value-added associates can identify wasted motions and use their lean training to improve the processes in their areas.

Waste of Making Defective Products (Rework)

With this type of waste, the problem is not the rework but the process that is causing the rework. Thus, the key question is, "What's causing the rework?" It is rarely a single person who makes a mistake; instead, it is usually a faulty system. This was an important point to make to the associates: The company understands that the majority of quality problems come from system problems, not individual problems. The Rudrey trainer used a recent example of rework from the facility, showing the rework and the process problem that made the rework necessary.

For a long time, Rudrey viewed rework as just another part of the process. It was an accepted part of the way things were done. Because of this mindset, the trainer had to spend considerable time discussing how Rudrey would now try to fix problems that caused rework, instead of allowing the rework to continue as a "normal" part of production. The trainer's most convincing argument for this change was reminding associates about the competition, market share, and profitability. By tying each of these to rework, she was able to show how costly this waste can be within the walls of the facility and beyond.

Going Forward

Rudrey knew before it started the facility-wide training that there would be a lot of pressure on management and the organization in general to take the information from the training sessions and run with it. In other words, the entire organization would have to commit to putting the information learned to good use. Obviously, management would have to assume the lead in this transition, if only to show that this was a serious commitment to a serious system change, not just another "flavor-of-month" endeavor leading nowhere. The trainer, for example, had said that management would now fix machines when they broke. For Rudrey management, this meant that broken machines would indeed be fixed. The repair, aside from improving production, would send a strong signal to the people working in the facility that the new program was not just a whim but a whole new way of doing things. Even employees most skeptical of management and change initiatives, would see that management is serious and that "lean" is not just another program that will disappear in a few months.

Management also recognized the need to encourage a lot of questioning on the part of hourly associates, even though some of the questions might be difficult or uncomfortable for management to answer. In the old days, management was rarely asked "Why?" about anything. The question was frowned upon and seen almost as insubordination. The only people who asked it were troublemakers. But in a lean manufacturing environment that fosters a culture of continuous improvement, asking questions is encouraged. Asking questions forces people to understand the processes happening on the floor and to notice each step, so managers, supervisors, and team leaders have to commit themselves to embracing questions. And to asking questions themselves.

To this end, after Lean 101 training concluded, Rudrey immediately posted a list of the seven forms of waste on a white board (see Figure 3-6) in each of the areas that had sent people to the training sessions

White Board

Seven Wastes	Name	Waste Found	Supervisor Signoff
Overproduction Waiting Transportation of material Processing Inventory Operator and machine motion Rework			

Figure 3-6.

and encouraged hourly associates to begin writing down forms of waste that they saw. Rudrey assigned supervisors to review the white board every shift to see whether or not any forms of waste had been noted and who had written them. The next step was having the appropriate person or people determine what was causing the waste, when it could be fixed, and what it would take to fix it.

Summing Up

- Realize that there will be some uncertainty about lean among associates and that this needs to be addressed.
- Be honest and forthcoming as to why lean manufacturing is being implemented.
- Describe the seven forms of manufacturing wastes in detail.
- Provide associates with a way to communicate the wastes that they identify.

CHAPTER 4

Workplace Organization

Rudrey, like other companies that successfully implement lean manufacturing systems, understood the importance of workplace organization. One objective of Rudrey's strategic training plan, therefore, was to introduce the value-added associates to workplace organization.

Rudrey had already assembled a continuous improvement team, consisting of individuals who had helped in previous improvement efforts. It was a reward-based team: If an associate helped improve the process and was freed up as a result, he or she was not laid off (as discussed in Chapter 3), but became a member of the continuous improvement team. This team was a group of hands-on implementers who played the lead role in implementing workplace organization as well as making other improvements in the facility.

6S Training

At Rudrey, workplace organization is called 6S and is modeled after the 5S system at Toyota. Translated into English, the 5Ss stand for "sort, straighten, shine, standardize, and sustain."[1] Rudrey's 6S model included a "safety" component. Each S serves a specific need and involves a specific function or activity:

- **Sorting** through an area to get rid of unneeded items
- **Straightening** up an area to improve organization, thus creating visual management
- **Shining** up an area until it's spotless
- **Standardizing** how all items are labeled and marked throughout the facility

---

1. See C. Marchwinski and J. Shook, eds. *Lean Lexicon*. Brookline, MA: Lean Enterprise Institute, 2003, p. 20.

- **Sustaining** workplace organization through a system of audits, everyday actions, and continuous improvement
- **Safety**, the top priority

When to Train

Rudrey had to determine when to institute 6S training for its associates. This was an important question, because Rudrey associates from individual departments or areas were already at different stages or levels of lean. Some were already working where some lean implementation had occurred, but had not yet been adequately trained. For this reason, the first people to train were those whose areas had already been organized with the 6S method. Once this group was trained, Rudrey planned to train the remaining hourly associates a day or two before the continuous improvement team came to their areas for the implementation.

Who Attended

The people attending each session of 6S training were the value-added associates, the team leader, the area supervisor, a Human Resources representative, and a member of the continuous improvement team. The trainer was, once again, the facility's Lean Coordinator.

Goals of the 6S One-Hour Workshop

The goals of the 6S training were as follows:

- Explain the six steps (or 6Ss) to an organized, safe workplace.
- Provide description and examples of each S.
- Present the 6S method as a systematic approach to workplace organization.

Sort

Sort is the first step in the 6S process. The objective of Sort is to clear an area of the many unneeded items that consume space with no purpose. Almost all people have something in their work area that they never use, and they are often not quite sure why it is there. Manufacturing plant team leaders and group leaders may simply keep items around because they don't want to throw them away. Odds are, these miscellaneous odds and ends in the manufacturing areas are just taking up space. Sorting means deciding what is needed and what is not needed, so that the unneeded items can be removed from the area.

Some items are obviously clutter, but Sorting is not always cut and dry. What, for example, should be done about items used so seldom that few people even know what they are? Weeding them out can be tricky, because one of them may suddenly be needed for a rarely performed process. Rudrey handled this situation in the following manner: If an item was used for every product or used frequently, the team created a place for it and stored it in the area. If an item was used only occasionally, Rudrey found a place to store it somewhere outside the area. Finally, unused items (or those thought unused) were designated red-tag items and place in a red-tag area for 2 weeks. After the 2 weeks, if no one asked about a particular item or noticed it was missing, the item in question was thrown away.

It is important for Operations to dispose of what it does not need. The production floor is used to add value to the product; it should not be a storage facility. Once, the area has been sorted, with every unneeded item removed, the second step in the process can begin.

Straighten

Straightening means organizing, identifying a place for everything, and putting everything in its proper place. Rudrey's straightening process can be summed up in this way:

- Everything needs a place.
- Every place needs to be clearly identified.
- All items must be moved to their designated places.
- Use visual controls to determine whether or not an item is in the wrong place.

Visual controls are critical to straightening an area, and Rudrey's visual management system had strict parameters. The trainer explained that Rudrey wanted someone with no previous knowledge of the processes to come in and see exactly what was happening in the facility. When the trainer made this statement, some associates were offended because the comment seemed to belittle their jobs. She quickly explained that the "someone" did not mean someone off the street, but referred to other associates, supervisors, support staff, and managers who worked in the facility every day. If a plant is set up with this in mind, all the people who work there will have a much easier time understanding their workplace and what goes on in that workplace.

Shine

The Shine step is about thoroughly cleaning the area. This is done the old-fashioned way, by getting out on the floor and cleaning everything by hand. A clean area has many benefits, most important of which is that cleanliness makes problems easier to see. If, for example, a machine is really dirty and is also leaking, the leak is difficult to spot. If the leak is noticed too late, it may cause major downtime. If the machine is clean, a leak will be obvious and the problem can be corrected before it becomes bad enough to stop production.

This deep dive into shining the facility should have to be done only once. After the initial cleaning, the area should require only simple, daily cleaning.

Standardize

Rudrey developed standards for how items should be labeled and marked. For example, colored tape is placed on the floor to designate the place for an item. Rudrey uses the following color codes for this purpose:

- Red = scrap
- Blue = incoming materials
- Green = empty container
- Yellow + black = hazardous material
- Brown = work-in-process
- Gray = finished goods

Areas where scrap is stored are marked on the floor with red tape, and areas with finished goods soon leaving the floor are marked on the floor with gray tape. This approach (and the color coding) is standardized throughout the facility. When an associate or supervisor changes areas, he or she does not have to learn a new system. Prior to implementing the system, Rudrey management set up a pilot area, where associates could view how the system looked and worked.

Sustain (and Improve)

Rudrey knew that organizing a workplace without a system in place to improve it and sustain improvement would lead back to disorganization. To prevent this regression, Rudrey planned to sustain and improve workplace organization through an auditing system that involved supervisors, team leaders, and associates.

The trainer explained that audits were not going to be used to detect wrongdoing; they would be used check the workplace to ensure that improvements were being sustained and that new ways to improve were being noted. This point had to be made because many companies, including Rudrey in its pre-lean days, had used audits solely to catch people doing something wrong. The best audits are not used for this purpose; instead, they exist for the purpose of improving workplace organization and making sure that best practices are being followed. Constantly monitoring areas and posting the resulting audit forms where everyone can see them ensures there are no secrets in this process and motivates people to raise their standards. Moreover, good audit forms are uncomplicated; as Figure 4-1 shows, they are simple, easy to complete, and easy to understand.

Safety

Rudrey management has always realized that workers cannot be productive and efficient if they are worried about getting hurt on the job, so safety is a priority in the Rudrey facility. Associates and management constantly ask, "Is the area/process safe?" and "What can be done to make the area/process safer?" Implementing workplace organization provided an additional tool to help ensure that the facility was

Rudrey 6S Audit Form

Date: _____

Area: _____

Auditor: _____

*If No is checked on any item, the area automatically recieves a 1 for that "S."
**For each NO, a corrective action needs to be developed and completed.
***Scores are 1–5 for each "S," Area Score is the total of the 6 "S" scores.

	Yes	No	Score for "S"
Sort			
Does everything in the area belong in the area?			
Is the red tag area well identified?			
Is there evidence that the red tag area is being utilized?			
Straighten			
Does every item in the area have a place?			
Is every place for an item identified?			
Are visual controls utilized to identify each place (tape, paint, etc.)?			
Is the tape on the floor in good shape?			
Shine			
Is the area clean?			
Are the machines in the area clean?			
Is the floor swept?			
Standardize			
Is the area following the facility standards?			
Sustain			
Are past audits posted in the area?			
Is there evidence that the audits are being used to improve?			
Safety			
Does the area appear to be free of obvious safety hazards?			
Are safety meetings being conducted on a regular basis?			
Is there evidence that open safety issues are being addressed?			
Area Score			

*5 = Outstanding; 4 = Above Expectations; 3 = Acceptable; 2 = Not Acceptable; 1 = Action Needed

Figure 4-1.

as safe as possible. Generally, a clean and organized area is far safer than a dirty and disorganized one, but constant vigilance is needed, even for areas that adhere to the other 5Ss.

Summing Up

- Clean and organized working environments promote safety, quality, and productivity.

- The goal of workplace organization training is not to make the associates experts in workplace organization, but to explain the methodology so that associates can assist in the implementation.

- In the training, stress that 6S is a step-by-step method.

- Try to schedule a workplace organization event a day or two after the training.

- Follow through with a standard cadence of audits (every day, every week, every shift, or whatever pattern best suits the needs of your facility).

CHAPTER 5

Value Stream Maps

As part of its lean initiative, Rudrey had been drawing value stream maps and placing them in manufacturing areas where associates could see them. What Rudrey had not done was to tell associates what the value stream maps meant. This caused some confusion on the floor: The maps were up, but the associates didn't know (or care) why they were there and assumed this was just another fly-by-night program that would disappear in a couple months.

Obviously, Rudrey management had to train the value-added associates to understand and use the value stream maps; the real question was about the extent of that training. Rudrey decided that engineers and management would continue to draw the value stream maps for the facility, so that associate training could focus on understanding and interpreting them. If, in the future, some associates expressed an interest in drawing value stream maps, Rudrey could provide additional training later.

Who Attended

The trainer planned a one-hour workshop to explain the key points of a value stream map, including its purpose. The engineer who drew the maps, along with a Human Resources representative, team leaders, and the group leader, also attended.

Goals of the Training

The goals of the one-hour value stream map workshop were as follows:

- Explain the purpose of the value stream map.
- Explain what a value stream map shows.
- Explain how value stream maps affect hourly associates.

The Purpose of a Value Stream Map

The value stream map, as Rudrey utilized it, had two main objectives: one was present focused, and the other was future focused.

Showing What Is Happening on the Production Floor

The first purpose of a value stream map is that it shows exactly what is happening on the production floor—not what the engineer thinks is happening or what the manager hopes is happening, but what actually is happening. As such, a value stream map provides a point of discussion about manufacturing activities. No one has to guess what is happening; the value stream map shows the actual process in its current state.

If you look at Figure 5-1,[1] you can see the material flow across the bottom of the map, showing various inventory levels between processes that slow lead time. The data boxes show labor, downtime, cycle time, and changeover time. Across the top, the map shows information flow. Materials[2] is at the top center of the map because that department is the hub of the process: It receives orders from customers, releases those orders to production, and orders raw material from suppliers.

The final item that Rudrey wanted its associates to see on the value stream map was the distinction between process time and lead time. (Lead time is often misunderstood as being the same as processing time.) Lead time is the time it takes raw material to go from the receiving door to the shipping door as finished goods. Processing time, on the other hand, is how long it actually takes to assemble or process a product. The two times can be very different. In Figure 5-1, the lead time is 20 days, and the processing time is only 112.4 seconds. The question that should arise here is why a product that takes only 112.4 seconds to produce is in the plant for 20 days. The answer is simple: waste and inefficiency in the system. Unfortunately, long lead time is very costly to an organization.

---

1. Methodology and symbols to develop the maps were taken from the book *Learning to See: Value-Stream Mapping to Create Value and Eliminate Muda* by M. Rother and J. Shook. Brookline, MA: The Lean Enterprise Institute, 1998.

2. Materials control can also be referred to as production control or production control and logistics (PC&L).

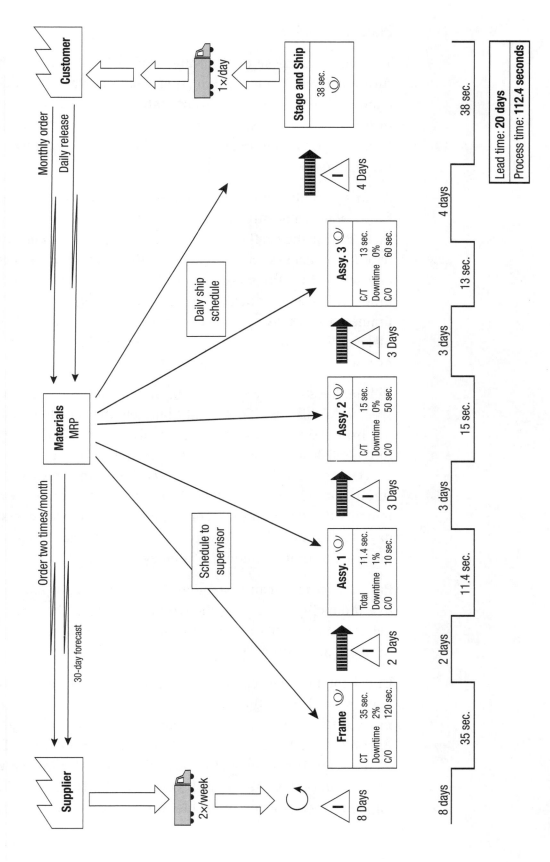

Figure 5-1.

Plans for the Future

The second purpose of the value stream map was to plan for the future. Just drawing a value stream map is wasteful because it communicates only the current state of the facility. The real value in drawing a value stream map is that it is the foundation of a future state value stream map, which gives a company a game plan for change.

A current state value stream map should look very different from a future state value stream map. One of the big differences between them is that they reflect a change from a push system to a pull system. In a push system, for example, the Frame area makes a product and sends it to Assembly 1 even if Assembly 1 has not requested the product. Loosely defined, a push system is a system that allows the Frame area to make whatever products it wants, when it wants to make it; Assembly 1 is going to get the product, whether it needs it or not.

In a pull system (see Figure 5-2), there is only one schedule per value stream. In this case, Stage and Ship gets the schedule and pulls product from Assembly's market. Assembly in turn sends a signal to Frame to replenish what was taken from its market by Stage and Ship. This process goes all the way back to Receiving, thus creating pull throughout the entire system. As the figure shows, processing time remains the same (112.4 seconds), but lead time decreases from 20 days to 4 days, 1 hour—a very big difference that can save the company a substantial amount of money.

Pull is vital to a lean system because it prevents Operations from overproducing or making the wrong product at the wrong time. It helps to ensure that Operations makes only what it needs, when it needs it, and in the right quantities.

Under the push system, every area received a schedule, so each knew what it needed for the week. This provided the opportunity to run many different parts. For example, if a schedule said that 100 A, 100 B, 100 C, and 100 D parts need to be made on Monday, Tuesday, Wednesday, Thursday, and Friday, the total order for the week for the line would be 500 A, 500 B, 500 C, and 500 D parts. To be "efficient," an area supervisor might decide to run a week's worth of A parts on

59

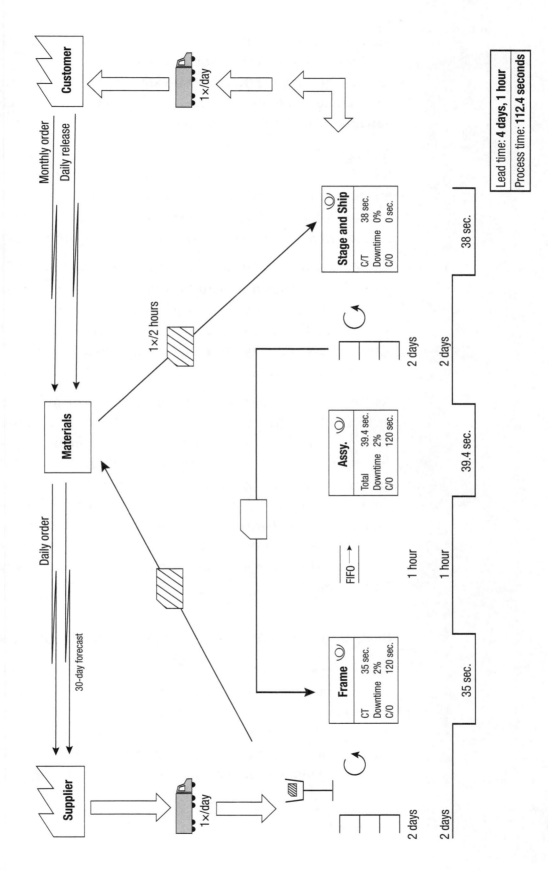

Figure 5-2.

Monday, putting off B parts until Tuesday. But if this "efficiency" is not based on a logical reason, it can cause major problems in the system: If, for example, the downstream area needs part B, but these parts are unavailable until the next day, the result is likely to be downtime, unplanned changeovers, and so on.

As Figure 5-2 illustrates, Rudrey made some significant plans for its future state. The facility went to one schedule per value stream and pulled through the remainder of its production process. Operations inserted a FIFO[3] lane to minimize inventory, and it substantially reduced lead time by combining the assembly areas.

Rudrey had what they called the 75, 2, 20 rule. Rudrey found that productivity doubled in value streams where lead time was reduced by 75 percent; moreover, the cost per product in these areas went down 20 percent. This was strong motivation to continually utilize the value stream maps and make sure that the associates understood the maps and their purpose.

As the trainer explained, value stream maps inspire change. Rudrey, in fact, followed its future state value stream maps with 30-, 60-, 90-day plans for implementing change. The maps also served as "reality check." If there was an idea to improve part of the process, managers could easily judge from future state maps whether the proposed change fit into the plan. If it did not, there was either something wrong with the map or with the change idea, and the map was amended or the change idea was shelved. But once associates understood the maps and their aim, most improvement ideas fit future plans.

How Value Stream Maps Affect Value-Added Associates

Value stream maps may not affect value-added associates every day, but the maps do provide information on the plans for the future, and that means associates are getting far more information than they have in the past. Rudrey management made a concerted effort to improve information flow, and value stream maps helped them do that. With the maps, value-added associates had information on progress in

---

3. FIFO is first in, first out

plant; they also had visual resources that made it easy for them to ask better, focused questions and suggest suitable changes.

Summing Up

- Utilize real maps that you have drawn in your facility.
- Walk the value stream on the production floor to make the classroom training real.
- Explain that value stream maps provide a game plan for change.

CHAPTER 6

Continuous (One-Piece) Flow

Continuous flow has the most significant impact on the way value-added associates perform their everyday processes, and Rudrey saw a definite need to train the hourly associates on the true meaning of continuous flow, one-piece flow, cellular manufacturing, value-added work, incidental work, and related concepts.

Not all of the Rudrey facility would be put into a cellular manufacturing layout, but the principles of continuous flow would be implemented throughout the entire facility. Already, Rudrey had started to see some significant benefits to utilizing continuous flow principles, especially in getting control of shopfloor processes. For this reason, the Rudrey training team carefully planned a strategic training initiative and developed a workshop that was approximately an hour in length.

Who Attended

Once again, Rudrey utilized the Lean Coordinator as the trainer. Supervisors and industrial engineers (sometimes called process engineers), deeply involved in continuous flow, and the HR representative attended all of the training sessions.

Goals of the Training

Rudrey set the following goals for the training:

- Explain continuous (one-piece) flow.
- Identify the three types of work motion.
- Define a work element.
- Explain how the number of associates needed is calculated.
- Explain standardized work and its importance.

Understanding Continuous (One-Piece) Flow

It can be difficult to explain one-piece flow to a group of people, and the training team had to create a workable process for conveying this information. The best solution was to use an example, which included a quick and simple simulation.

The trainer began the workshop by asking for four volunteers, who were asked to sit at a table in the front of the room, facing the rest of the class. The trainer gave each of the volunteers a pen and then placed a stack of paper on the table. Participants were asked to write their names on ten different pieces of paper and then pass the entire batch of ten pages to the person to their left. The trainer asked another volunteer from the class to time how long it took to get four different names on each of the ten sheets.

The simulation was run and timed. The audience watched the batch production, and then the time was written on the board. The trainer than asked the class, "What did you see? What do you think? How much quicker do you think the process would be if each person wrote his or her name on one page, and then passed the page to the left?"

The simulation was repeated, but this time the first participant wrote his name on one page and then passed it to the left, with the next participant doing the same, and so on. The timer timed the new process and recorded the results on the board. The time difference was radically different; the new process was much faster and clearly showed the class the benefits of one-piece flow. After thanking the participants, the trainer continued the workshop by explaining the theory behind the simulation.

The associates had heard a lot about "pull," but it had never been explained to them until they attended the session on value stream maps. Rudrey management decided that this training session should include an in-depth explanation that would increase and reinforce the associates' knowledge of pull. As noted in the previous chapter, in a pull system, you build only what is needed, instead of building up inventory. The system is based on replenishment, as shown in Figure 6-1. Rudrey used this figure to explain to associates that the production scheduling on the floor was going to become much less complicated because of the pull system.

Future

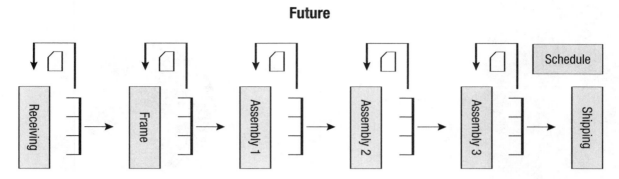

Figure 6-1.

In this figure, you can see that only Shipping is going to get a schedule. Shipping then pulls what it needs from Assembly 3's market. In turn, Assembly 3 gets a pull signal, letting it know that Shipping has pulled the product. This signal tells Assembly 3 what it needs to make next. To complete the pull sequence, Assembly 3 has to pull from Assembly 2's market. Then Assembly 2 receives the signal, letting it know what was pulled and what it needs to pull from Assembly 1 to make the order. With this system, there is no guessing about what needs to be made and when.

When you hit this point in the training, keep in mind that the front-line supervisors' job goes through a significant change during a lean transformation, and most supervisors are uncomfortable with the change until they see the benefits. See Chapter 9 for more information on training supervisors as you move to lean.

Reviewing the Three Types of Work Motion

Up until this point, Rudrey had discussed only two types of work motion: value-added or non-value-added. However, there is a third type of work motion, which is incidental motion.[1] In its training, Rudrey utilized specific examples of its processes to illustrate each of the three types. (See Figure 6-2 for an overview of the three types of work motion.)

---

1. The three types of work motion are taken from M. Rother and R. Harris, *Creating Continuous Flow: An Action Guide for Managers, Engineers & Production Associates.* Brookline, MA: The Lean Enterprise Institute, 2001.

Types of Work Motion

- Wasted work motions
- Incidental work motions
- Value-added work motions

Figure 6-2.

Value-added work motion, of course, adds value to the product. An example of value-added work is bolting one part to another.

The second type of work motion is waste. An example of wasted work motion is walking to a finished goods bin or waiting for a product.

The third and final work motion is called incidental work motion. This work motion is something that the associate has to do, but it does not add value to the product. An example of this type of work motion is getting a screwdriver. The associate must have the screwdriver in hand to drive the screw, but getting the screwdriver does not add value to the product.

It is important for associates to understand each of the three types of work motion because this enables them to discover and eliminate waste. Figure 6-2 shows that waste is a very big part of the pie in traditional manufacturing, but continuous flow makes it possible to eliminate waste and greatly reduce incidental work motions. When this is accomplished, the value-added portion of the circle becomes a great deal bigger, which can lead to greater profitability for the company.

Describing a Work Element

How do you identify a value-added, incidental, or wasteful work motion? The first step is to separate all the steps that it takes to produce a product into work elements. A work element is a piece of work that can be easily transferred from one associate to another. For example, getting a screwdriver and driving a screw is a work element, but simply getting a screwdriver is not a work element because it cannot be passed to another associate.

Understanding each work element is the job of industrial engineers, who will likely be standing around with clipboards, writing down the work elements and timing them. Once the work elements are collected, they will then be classified as value-added work elements, incidental work elements, or wasteful work elements. The Rudrey trainer explained that there was no need for the associates to feel nervous about having these engineers document the work elements. She explained, once again, that the purpose of this work was to make the company better, not to catch someone doing something wrong.

This was also a good time to point out that engineers have an obligation to tell associates what they are doing. In a lean system, there is no reason to have any secrets. It is shopfloor courtesy for someone coming in to observe a job to tell the associates what is being observed and why, even if the explanation is as simple as, "I am getting the work elements for this process."

The next step in the process is to time the work elements, which probably means people standing around with stopwatches. Again, there is no need for the associate to be nervous; stopwatches (and the engineers who will be holding them) are there only to make the company more efficient.

Calculating the Number of Needed Associates

Engineers need to time the work elements to determine the number of associates needed to meet customer demand. This is done by taking the total time that it takes to do the process without the waste and dividing that number by the takt time (discussed in Chapter 3). See Figure 6-3.

Before lean, assembly and manufacturing processes were inefficient, often staffed with too many associates engaged in wasted movements. With lean, the machines used to assemble or manufacture one product will likely be moved closer together, something Rudrey stressed during its training sessions. In the past, Rudrey had processes scattered throughout the plant, an inefficient setup that involved too many people and too many wasteful motions. By moving machines closer

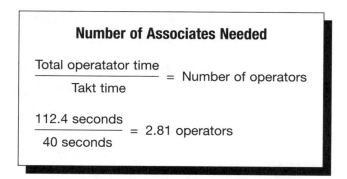

Figure 6-3.

together and running one-piece flow, Rudrey was able to run processes with the correct number of associates and fewer wasteful motions. Figure 6-4 illustrates the new arrangement, and Figure 6-5 illustrates the new walk patterns that emerged once the new pattern was in place.

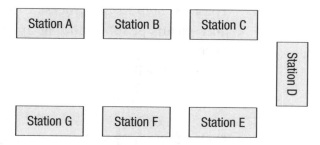

Figure 6-4.

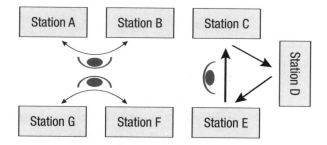

Figure 6-5.

Seeing the Value of Standardized Work

For the last portion of the training, the trainer asked, "Is there one best method to produce a product?" The majority of the class participants said that there is no one best method. The Rudrey trainer disagreed, explaining that "best" was part of a continuous improvement process. If, for example, the first shift associate is employing the current best method, but the second shift associate finds a better method, that method becomes the new best method. First shift will have to change to the new best method, which becomes the new standard.

Standardized work is making the product the same way every time. This is one of the foundations of a lean production system. If the associate does the work the same way every time, the company can rest assured that quality will be consistently better; if the product is built a different way every time, quality will likely be erratic. Rudrey's commitment to this concept became a facility mantra: "There is no improvement without standards to improve on!"

The final component of continuous flow training focused on two questions: "Who develops the standardized work?" and "Who does Rudrey rely on to continually improve the standardized work, after it's developed?" The answers to both questions encapsulate the content of the session.

- "Who develops the standardized work?" The individual or group of individuals (usually industrial engineers, along with a great deal of input from the value-added associates) that determine the work elements, time the elements, and then determine the number of associates needed to produce the product.

- "Who does Rudrey rely on to improve the standardized work continually, after it's developed?" The value-added associate.

Summing Up

- Use a simulation to show the value of one-piece flow.
- Explain three different types of work motion.
- Emphasize why people will see the engineers on the floor and that the input of these engineers is valuable to the process.
- Stress the importance of doing the job the same way every time (that is, doing standardized work).

CHAPTER 7

Lean Materials Delivery Systems

Although the hourly associates' part in a lean materials delivery system is relatively small, it is nevertheless important. To make sure the role of the value-added associates was well defined and well understood, Rudrey management developed the training workshop discussed in this chapter.

Who Attended

The Lean Coordinator served as trainer. Value-added associates, team leaders, area supervisors, the manager of the Materials department for the facility, and an HR representative attended the sessions.

Goals for the Training

Goals for the training included the following:

- Define and explain the plan for every part (PFEP).
- Define and explain a purchased parts market, a work-in-process (WIP) market, and a finished goods market.
- Define and explain pull signals, with an emphasis on the value-added associates' role in the system.
- Define and explain the materials delivery route.

The Plan for Every Part (PFEP)[1]

The plan for every part (PFEP) is a database for every part in the facility. It holds the part number, where the part is used, the volume, container size, the number of parts in each container, supplier information, and so on. An example is shown in Figure 7-1.

1. Harris, et al. *Making Materials Flow: A Lean Material-Handling Guide for Operations, Production Control, and Engineering Professionals.* Brookline, MA: The Lean Enterprise Institute, 2003.

72

PFEP

Assumptions: Weekly Delivery = 5 days shipment size
Daily Delivery = 1 day shipment size
Monthly Delivery = 20 days shipment size

Part #	Description	Daily Usage	Usage Location	Storage Location	Order Frequency	Supplier	Supplier City	Supplier State	Supplier Country	Container Type	Container Weight	1 Part Weight
16598	Cab	1000	Cell 11	Supermarket	Daily	Cab's R us	Murrells Inlet	SC	US	EXP.	5	0.0500
16579	Hood	1000	Cell 11	Supermarket	Weekly	R&A Inc.	Georgetown	SC	US	RET.	5	0.0500
16656	Front frame	1000	Cell 11	Cell 12	4× day	Cell 11	In plant		US	RET.	Internal skid	
16224	Link nut	4000	Cell 11	Supermarket	2× week	G&F Corporation	Noblesville	IN	US	RET.	1	0.2000
17777	Front end	1000	Cell 11	Supermarket	Daily	Ideas for Molding	Summerville	SC	US	EXP.	5	1.0000
18888	Bed assembly	1000	Cell 11	Supermarket	Weekly	Beds Here	Andrews	SC	US	EXP.	3	2.0000
14998	Back/middle frame	1000	Cell 11	Cell 10	4× day	Cell 10	In plant		US	RET.	Internal skid	
13265	Tail pipe	2000	Cell 11	Supermarket	3× week	Pipes 'n Such	Florence	SC	US	EXP.	1	1.0000
12567	Hose clamp	2000	Cell 11	Supermarket	Weekly	Moon Mfg.	Anderson	IN	US	EXP.	1	0.0001

Part #	Width	Height	Usage per Assembly	Hourly Usage	Standard Pack Quantity	Packs Used Per Hour	Shipment Size	Carrier	Transit Time	# of Cards in Loop	Supplier Performance
16598	6	6	1	125	125	1	5 days	Local Trucking	3 days	3	5
16579	6	6	1	125	125	1	5 days	Local Trucking	2 days	3	2
16656	Internal skid	Internal skid	1	125	125	1	1 day	Internal	5 minutes	3	4
16224	4	4	4	500	100	5	5 days	Local Trucking	2 days	15	1
17777	12	6	1	125	125	1	20 days	USF	2 days	3	1
18888	12	12	1	125	25	5	20 days	Local Trucking	3 days	15	1
14998	Internal skid	Internal skid	1	125	25	5	1 day	Internal	5 minutes	15	1
13265	12	6	2	250	125	2	5 days	Local Trucking	2 days	6	1
12567	6	6	2	250	125	2	5 days	Local Trucking	1 day	6	1

Supplier Performance: Excellent 1, Good 2, Fair 3, Bad 4

Figure 7-1.

Only one person in the facility has the authority to change the PFEP, and that is the PFEP manager. However, although no one else is permitted to change the document, anyone can view, sort, or print it. All hourly associates with questions about a part have access to the PFEP. The PFEP is on designated computers throughout the plant at Rudrey, so the Rudrey trainer demonstrated and created hands-on activities for associates to practice calling up and using the document on those computer stations.

The Purchased Parts Market and WIP[2]

The next important element of lean materials delivery system training is the purchased parts market. As the trainer explained, in the past, Rudrey had difficulty controlling the purchased parts inventory, because the parts were scattered throughout the facility in a disorganized manner. To get better control of purchased parts, Rudrey implemented a purchased parts market—that is, a clean, well-organized storage point in which there is a specific location for each item, including well-identified minimum and maximum levels. The part will be in this location today, tomorrow, next week, and so on, until a reason arises to move the part or the entire market moves.

A purchased parts market is much more than a warehouse or an off-site facility because it is set up to control inventory and efficiently supply the value-added associate with parts. The trainer used "before and after" pictures to show how a purchased parts market works. (See Figures 7-2 and 7-3). In Figure 7-2, material is brought directly from the receiving dock and taken to the production floor. The process is complex, difficult, and disorganized. Figure 7-3 shows what the facility looks like after a purchased parts market is implemented. All purchased parts are put in one area, a central location where controlling the inventory levels is not only possible, but also relatively simple. Notice that the cluttered areas in Figure 7-2 are clean in Figure 7-3. The Rudrey trainer also made sure to convey to the associates that purchased parts are a significant cost to the company and that managing purchased parts more efficiently reduces that cost.

---

2. Ibid.

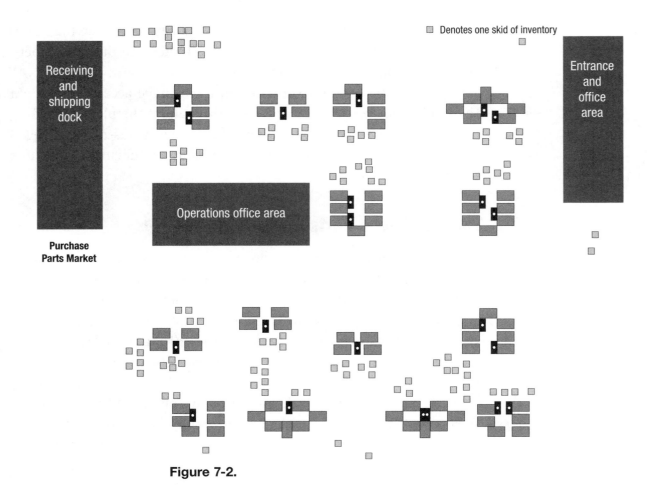

Figure 7-2.

The trainer also discussed markets for products made and completed in house or work-in-process (WIP), indicating that those markets would remain at the point of manufacture, so they can be managed by the producing department. The finished goods and WIP markets operate the same way as the purchased parts market and are arranged with the same methodology in mind. The markets are clean and well organized, with a specific location for each item.

Pull Signals[3] and the Value-Added Associates

By now, the hourly associates had an understanding of the PFEP and markets but were not entirely certain of their role in the system. Rudrey explained the process this way: "We determined what pur-

---

3. Ibid.

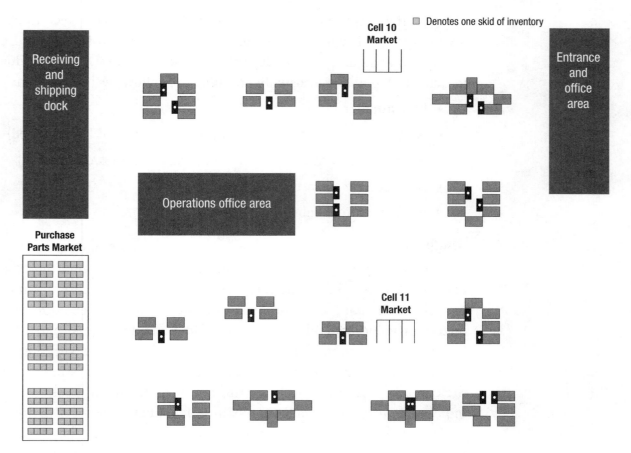

Figure 7-3.

chased parts we have with the PFEP, and then we put all the purchased parts in one well organized place—a purchased parts market. Now we have to utilize a system so that the value-added associates can tell the purchased parts market what parts they need. To do this, we're going to utilize pull signals, in the form of kanban cards, as the informational link between the shop floor and the purchased parts market."

The training includes sample pull signals (kanban cards), along with the following explanations of what a pull signal is:

- The authority to move material
- Completely visual
- Color-coded by route and department to facilitate faster sorting and loading in the purchased parts market
- Easily bar-coded, which can assist in ordering from suppliers

The Materials department also utilizes the kanban cards to keep track of inventory; that is why the kanban cards are numbered. Materials also relies on pull signals that let department associates know what product to deliver. A pull signal usually contains the following information:

- Part number
- Area used (this is the area to which the part will be delivered)
- Area stored in market (to facilitate easy location of the part)
- Minimum level in the market
- Kanban card number

A pull signal is the way associates tell the purchased parts market what parts they need. When the associate gets ready to pull the first part out of a box, he or she removes the signal (in this case, a kanban card) from the parts box and places the signal in a holder. To minimize non-value-added handling, the holder should be less than 12 inches from the container from which it is removed. It is very important to place the signal in the holder when the first part is pulled from the container, or associates may run out of materials. It is also very important not to place pull signals in holders before associates are ready to use the first piece out of the container, because then too much material will be delivered. Whenever a pull signal is placed in a holder, it means that more product has been ordered from the market to be delivered to the operator. If pull signals are not handled properly, the entire facility can be affected.

The Route[4]

The final point in the lean materials delivery training was to discuss the actual route. To illustrate the need for a timed delivery route run by a tugger,[5] the trainer asked the question: "Which is better, a taxi or a bus?" The trainer explained that a taxi drives around looking for a fare, finds one, takes the passenger directly to where he or she wants to go, and then charges the passenger a fare based on the distance traveled. On the other hand, a bus operates on a timed schedule or route: The

---

4. Ibid.

5. A tugger is a motorized vehicle designed to pull multiple carts of various material as opposed to a forklift, which carries one pallet of one part number.

bus shows up at the same place every hour, dropping off passengers and picking up new passengers. Each passenger pays the same fee.

Rudrey originally moved much of its material like a taxi, which meant moving only one part number at a time with forklifts that were generally empty half the time. The company decided to change to a bus route system, which meant making a shift from forklift to a tugger making multiple stops every hour, delivering products, and picking up kanban cards. The tugger, like the bus, is more efficient and more cost effective.

The Future of Lean Materials Delivery Systems

What can the associates expect to see in the future? Rudrey put together a set of slides that communicated the Materials future vision for the facility. Each slide presented one of the following features of Rudrey's future:

- One purchased parts market, which will be located near Receiving
- Mini WIP markets near points of manufacture
- One finished goods market near Shipping
- Mini WIP markets located along aisles to facilitate a timed delivery system
- Cells and manufacturing areas positioned to facilitate materials delivery
- Controlled materials delivery traffic, including one-way aisles and two-way aisles
- Forklifts restricted to Shipping and Receiving areas
- Materials delivery routes support specific areas of the plant, not specific departments

Summing Up

- Make sure associates understand how important their use of the kanban card is to the success of the system.
- Explain the big picture of the materials delivery system so that the associates see their vital role.

CHAPTER 8

Creating a Flexible Workforce

As your company implements lean manufacturing systems, you will come to value flexible employees, because a flexible workforce allows your manufacturing system to react to customer demand. Flexible employees are those with the capability to perform at many different workstations in a manufacturing area. For example, an employee able to complete work at each of six stations in a given area to takt time[1] (with exceptional quality) is flexible.

Rudrey knew that the more flexible its workforce, the better the manufacturing system, and the more the system could continually improve. For this reason, Rudrey management wanted every employee in a given team to be capable of meeting takt time and quality standards for every process for which that team was responsible. This was the short-term goal (1 year) for Rudrey; the company's long-term goal (3 years) was to have associates (team members) be proficient at every process, not only in their respective teams but also in their group. (A group may be composed of three to six manufacturing teams in the Rudrey facility, depending on the complexity, volume, and difficulty, of the manufacturing areas themselves.)

Rudrey management and HR decided that it would be HR's responsibility to facilitate the development of a flexible workforce. The HRD began developing a strategic plan to train the workforce in order to meet these goals. To develop its strategic plan, Rudrey revisited the questions that had been asked when the company developed other training programs: "who, what, when, where, and how?"

---

1. Takt time is the customer demand rate. This is the rate that a company needs to produce to meet customer demand without overproducing. See Chapter 3 for details.

Who Needs to Be Trained and in Which Areas?

The answer to the "who" question was simple: Every associate on the production floor and every member of a team was to be trained to become proficient in every process of that team. This, however, led to another question: "What is the current level of proficiency of the associates in the facility?" In other words, what was the starting point for change, and which associates could already do all the processes within the team?

To answer this question, Rudrey leaders reviewed other successfully completed initiatives. Chapter 7, for example, explains how Rudrey developed the Plan for Every Part (PFEP) when Rudrey was developing its materials delivery routes. When creating a materials delivery route, the Materials department first had to understand current state: what parts were needed, how many parts were needed, and so on. The PFEP accomplished this goal. Operations had begun its implementation the same way, by drawing current state value stream maps (see Chapter 5). Drawing on these experiences, Rudrey's HRD decided to use the same approach for flexibility training, that is, to determine the current state of employee flexibility. To accomplish this, Rudrey created a training matrix for each group comprising three to six teams.

Rudrey's training matrix enabled the company to assess the abilities of every employee in the facility (that is, which processes each employee could complete proficiently), and then to use that information to begin an on-the-job training program to increase and improve flexibility.

The Rudrey Training Matrix

After gathering the necessary information, Rudrey entered it in the matrix. The filled-in matrix showed, at a glance, who knew how to do what and at what level of proficiency. At the same time, it showed who needed training (or additional training) in specific processes. Figure 8-1 shows a blank matrix template; Figure 8-2 illustrates an evolving matrix, with names of associates and other relevant information inserted.

As Figure 8-2 illustrates, the first item inserted on the matrix is the group name or number. The next item is the group's location (or address) in the facility, which makes it easy to identify and locate the

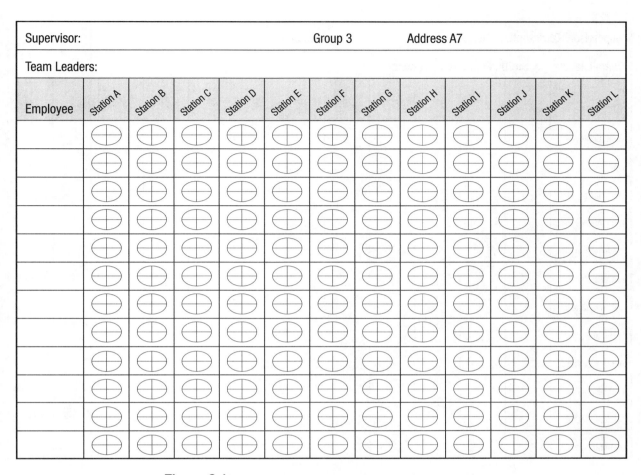

Figure 8-1.

group. The group leader and team leaders are listed at the top of the matrix, just above the list of workstations in the group; names of associates, listed by team, are in the left-hand column.

Identifying Training Quadrants

Each circle in the matrix shows the level of training of each associate involved in the process. There are four quadrants per circle, and each quadrant represents specific requirements. Among these requirements are standard generic items (such as understands exits, emergency procedure, and so on). Specific items required at specific workstations are also included. For example, Quadrant 1 (see Figure 8-3) lists safety requirements as well as basic knowledge requirements related to standardized work and quality issues.

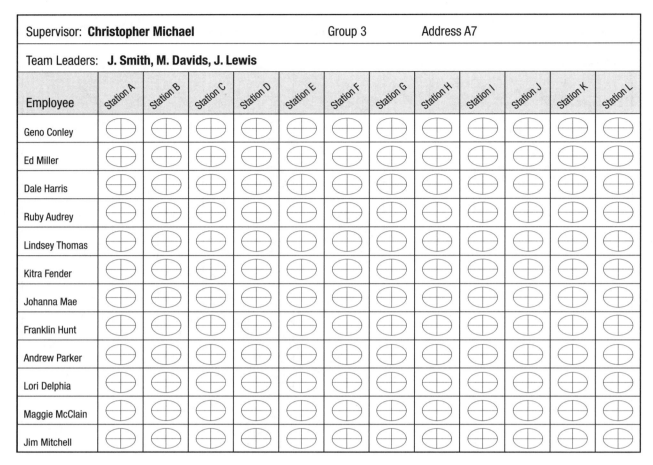

Supervisor: **Christopher Michael**						Group 3		Address A7			
Team Leaders: **J. Smith, M. Davids, J. Lewis**											
Employee	Station A	Station B	Station C	Station D	Station E	Station F	Station G	Station H	Station I	Station J	Station K	Station L
Geno Conley	⊕	⊕	⊕	⊕	⊕	⊕	⊕	⊕	⊕	⊕	⊕	⊕
Ed Miller	⊕	⊕	⊕	⊕	⊕	⊕	⊕	⊕	⊕	⊕	⊕	⊕
Dale Harris	⊕	⊕	⊕	⊕	⊕	⊕	⊕	⊕	⊕	⊕	⊕	⊕
Ruby Audrey	⊕	⊕	⊕	⊕	⊕	⊕	⊕	⊕	⊕	⊕	⊕	⊕
Lindsey Thomas	⊕	⊕	⊕	⊕	⊕	⊕	⊕	⊕	⊕	⊕	⊕	⊕
Kitra Fender	⊕	⊕	⊕	⊕	⊕	⊕	⊕	⊕	⊕	⊕	⊕	⊕
Johanna Mae	⊕	⊕	⊕	⊕	⊕	⊕	⊕	⊕	⊕	⊕	⊕	⊕
Franklin Hunt	⊕	⊕	⊕	⊕	⊕	⊕	⊕	⊕	⊕	⊕	⊕	⊕
Andrew Parker	⊕	⊕	⊕	⊕	⊕	⊕	⊕	⊕	⊕	⊕	⊕	⊕
Lori Delphia	⊕	⊕	⊕	⊕	⊕	⊕	⊕	⊕	⊕	⊕	⊕	⊕
Maggie McClain	⊕	⊕	⊕	⊕	⊕	⊕	⊕	⊕	⊕	⊕	⊕	⊕
Jim Mitchell	⊕	⊕	⊕	⊕	⊕	⊕	⊕	⊕	⊕	⊕	⊕	⊕

Figure 8-2.

Quadrant 1: Associate Knows the Job

- Associate understands all safety concerns and methods. ☑
- Standard work: Operator understands and correctly performs standardized work. ☑
- Associate understands what to do if there is a quality problem. ☑
- Associate understands where exits are. ☑
- Associate understands what to do in case of emergency. ☑
- Associate understands specific roles and responsibilities to materials system. ☑

Miscellaneous (a place for items deemed necessary for specific process):

_____

Figure 8-3.

Quadrant 2 determines whether or not an associate can do all of the work at the workstation, utilizing standardized work (see Figure 8-4). Rudrey's Operations department believed that associates should master a job first and worry about meeting takt time only after attaining excellent quality. The idea here was that proficiency and attention to quality provided a sound foundation. Once associates were comfortable with the correct way to do each process, they could work their way up to doing the processes to takt time.

Quadrant 2: Associate Can Perform the Job

- Associate performs the job, ✓ utilizing standardized work correctly. ☑

- Associate can do the entire job without assistance from the trainer. ☑

- Associate can reasonably recognize quality problems. ☑

Figure 8-4

Quadrant 3 (see Figure 8-5) was a critical step in the training progression; once completed, it meant that the associate could perform processes on their own without direct supervision or oversight by a team leader correctly to takt time.

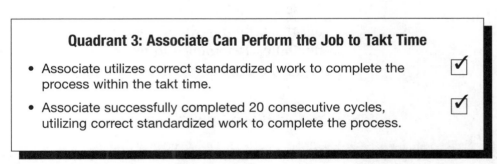

Quadrant 3: Associate Can Perform the Job to Takt Time

- Associate utilizes correct standardized work to complete the process within the takt time. ☑

- Associate successfully completed 20 consecutive cycles, utilizing correct standardized work to complete the process. ☑

Figure 8-5

When an associate reached the fourth quadrant of a process, he or she reached the Rudrey goal line. As Figure 8-6 shows, the quadrant represents mastery of process, time, and quality. In the example, the associate has successfully completed ten consecutive periods (that is, portions of a workday) to takt time without building a single defective part.

> **Quadrant 4: Associate Is Proficient at the Job**
>
> • Associate has operated the station to takt time and without
>   a defect for 10 consecutive periods.

Figure 8-6

Setting Goals

After Rudrey decided what its optimal flexible workforce should be, management needed to set goals to reach that optimal state. Each of the four goals Rudrey management formulated focus on Quadrant 4 of the training matrix:

- Get 100 percent of associates to Quadrant 4 in every process in their team within the year.
- Get 25 percent of associates to Quadrant 4 on every process in their group within 1 year.
- Get 75 percent of associates to Quadrant 4 on every process in their group within 2 years.
- Get 100 percent of associates to Quadrant 4 on every process in their group within 3 years.

These were lofty goals motivated by a lofty purpose: By accomplishing them, Rudrey would transform its workforce into a powerhouse of flexibility. Determined to make this happen, management and HR began working on a specific training process.

Completing On-Site Training Sheets

With the training matrix, Rudrey had developed a standard approach to evaluating who was trained and ready to work at each process. At this point the company created a training sheet for individual workstations, which would show the progress of each associate on each job. (See Figure 8-7.) The sheet utilized the original matrix quadrants, tailored to specific work functions in each area.

Specific requirements were listed for each workstation. Each training sheet included signature lines for trainers and associates in training as

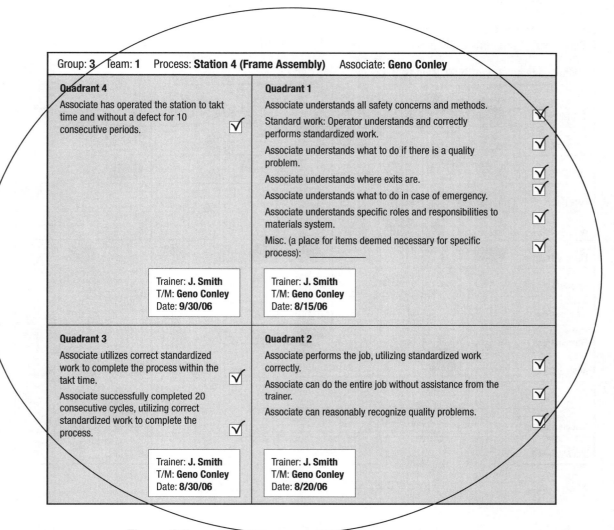

Group: **3** Team: **1** Process: **Station 4 (Frame Assembly)** Associate: **Geno Conley**

Quadrant 4

Associate has operated the station to takt time and without a defect for 10 consecutive periods. ☑

Trainer: **J. Smith**
T/M: **Geno Conley**
Date: **9/30/06**

Quadrant 1

Associate understands all safety concerns and methods. ☑

Standard work: Operator understands and correctly performs standardized work. ☑

Associate understands what to do if there is a quality problem. ☑

Associate understands where exits are. ☑

Associate understands what to do in case of emergency. ☑

Associate understands specific roles and responsibilities to materials system. ☑

Misc. (a place for items deemed necessary for specific process): _____ ☑

Trainer: **J. Smith**
T/M: **Geno Conley**
Date: **8/15/06**

Quadrant 3

Associate utilizes correct standardized work to complete the process within the takt time. ☑

Associate successfully completed 20 consecutive cycles, utilizing correct standardized work to complete the process. ☑

Trainer: **J. Smith**
T/M: **Geno Conley**
Date: **8/30/06**

Quadrant 2

Associate performs the job, utilizing standardized work correctly. ☑

Associate can do the entire job without assistance from the trainer. ☑

Associate can reasonably recognize quality problems. ☑

Trainer: **J. Smith**
T/M: **Geno Conley**
Date: **8/20/06**

Figure 8-7.

well as a line for the date each quadrant's requirements were successfully completed. These training sheets were stored in a binder under or near the Rudrey training matrix posted in the area. As Figure 8-8 shows, the original matrix was updated as quadrants were partially or entirely completed by associates in training.

Training Associates on All the Processes in a Group

Developing and completing the Rudrey training matrix let Rudrey see which associates were trained in which processes and what training was needed to meet its goals. In and of itself, however, the matrix did not, actually provide any training or develop any skills. Moreover,

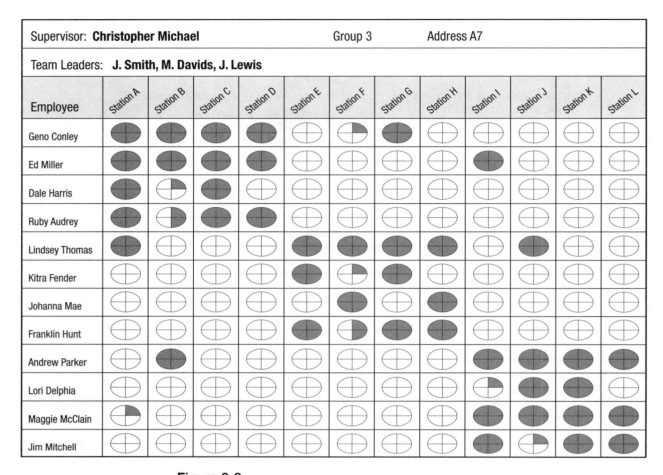

Figure 8-8.

while it was a helpful tool for identifying what people knew how to do and what they should learn, it did not adequately address the overarching goal that Rudrey had set: ✓ creating a flexible workforce.

Rudrey had to develop a way to train associates so that they could perform more processes, not just the processes they were performing in their current state. The first step was to determine who was going to train the associates and how they were going to be trained. Common sense dictated that the best method of training the employees would be on-the-job training because the only way to master doing standardized work to takt time was to do it. For this reason, the idea of classroom training was quickly abandoned: This flexibility training would occur on the floor.

The decision to train on the floor proved successful. Training could occur simultaneously in different areas or move from one area to another quickly. On-the-job training was effective as well as efficient: People would learn while doing (which meant actual work would be performed), and each group could train someone every day. Most importantly, because each group in the plant would be playing a role in the process of training and developing a flexible workforce, it would strengthen ties between teams and groups and promote a better understanding of what was happening in other areas or departments.

Who Does the Training—and When?

Something was missing in the Rudrey plan, and that was *who* was going to do the training and *when* that person (or those people) would train. Rudrey's HR department consulted with Operations and the lean coordinator, and the consultation produced a simple answer to both questions. The team leaders were already in Quadrant 4 and had enough knowledge and skill of the process(es) in their areas to train associates. Their schedules were also flexible enough to allow at least one team leader to train at least one period everyday.

Rudrey's workday was divided into four periods. The first period was from start time (7:00 A.M.) to the first break (8:45 A.M.). After this period, the workforce rotated; those who were trained on other processes would move to a different process they could successfully operate (ergonomics were carefully considered when the rotating pattern was developed). The second period was from 9:00 A.M. to lunch (11:00 A.M.). Again, after this period, associates rotated to another process in their team. The third period was 11:30 A.M. to second break (2:00 P.M.). Associates again rotated after this period. The fourth period was 2:15 to the end of the day (3:30 P.M.).

The only times associates at Rudrey rotated was after first break, lunch break, and afternoon break. This rotation plan gave the processes more stability than the every-hour rotation plan the company had previously used. (HR, in consultation with Operations, had made this change in the rotation policy after realizing the disruption in flow that hourly rotations caused.) Within this new rotation pattern, Rudrey's Operations department felt it was possible for a team leader in a group to train someone at least one period per day. Other team leaders in the same group could assist the designated trainers by covering their duties during training times. The HR department was going to play a significant support role in this training initiative. To begin the process, HR agreed to provide the Rudrey training matrix to each area, including the associates in the area, the group leaders, and team leaders as well. Although customized to fit the work of specific areas, the matrix would be standardized so that no matter which area someone was in, he or she would be able to understand what the matrix was showing.

In addition, HR designed and scheduled a training session to explain to operators what the training matrix was and how it affected them. The Lean Coordinator would conduct the hour-long session.

Executing the Details

Rudrey had learned that the best way to implement a new system was to jump in and begin, so it launched the new training program almost immediately. Human Resources and Operations did not have all the answers, but they knew that many valuable lessons would be learned along the way.

Planning Daily Training

The actual time of day for training varied from area to area. Some teams and groups were very busy at morning startup; other teams and groups were busiest near the end of the day. To accommodate this, HR worked with Operations to develop a training schedule that would work for each group without significant disruption. For example, Group Three would train an associate every day during second period, while Group Two would train an associate every day during fourth period.

Regardless of the details, management at the Rudrey facility wanted assurance that training was happening every day. Daily training, in management's opinion, equaled daily improvement for the facility as a whole. Figure 8-9 shows a detailed plan developed for Group Three. Note that a training session is scheduled for the second period of each weekday, rotated among stations.

Beginning on a Small Scale

In Rudrey's nonlean past, employees at the facility had seen many different programs come and go. The associates, team leaders, and the

April						
Sunday	Monday	Tuesday	Wednesday	Thursday	Friday	Saturday
1	2 Period 2 D. Harris Station B	3 Period 2 K. Fender Station F	4 Period 2 L. Delphia Station I	5 Period 2 D. Harris Station B	6 Period 2 K. Fender Station F	7
8	9 Period 2 L. Delphia Station I	10 Period 2 D. Harris Station B	11 Period 2 K. Fender Station F	12 Period 2 L. Delphia Station I	13 Period 2 D. Harris Station B	14
15	16 Period 2 K. Fender Station F	17 Period 2 L. Delphia Station I	18 Period 2 D. Harris Station B	19 Period 2 K. Fender Station F	20 Period 2 L. Delphia Station I	21
22	23 Period 2 D. Harris Station B	24 Period 2 K. Fender Station F	25 Period 2 L. Delphia Station I	26 Period 2 D. Harris Station B	27 Period 2 K. Fender Station F	28
29	30 Period 2 D. Harris Station C					

Figure 8-9.

supervisors (group leaders) had participated in just about every one of these initiatives and were understandably skeptical of new initiatives. Rudrey wanted to make sure that flexibility training was taken seriously and met its goals. Facility managers also wanted associates to see that the company was working to develop their skills.

To reinforce this focus on individual value and improvement, Rudrey's HR department decided to begin training on a small scale rather than on the plant level. The training would begin with a model group that included just three teams. The group comprised a total of twelve associates and three team leaders (four associates and one leader per team) and one group leader. Figure 8-10 shows a simple organizational chart of the group.

Human Resources planned to use this group to roll out the entire program. The first step was to post the Rudrey training matrix and complete it in its current state. Human Resources also provided training quadrant sheets for the area workstations.

Group Organizational Chart

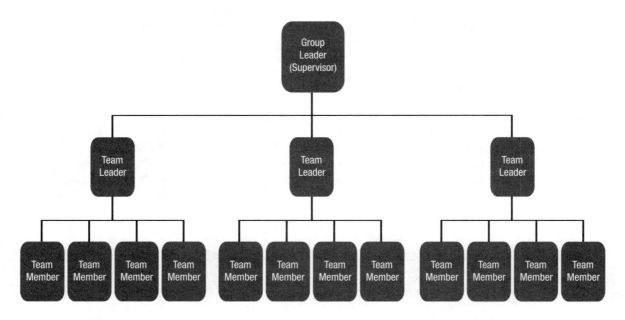

Figure 8-10.

Working with team leaders and the group leader, HR decided that the second period would be the optimal time for training. In addition, they decided to rotate the trainers (the team leaders). Team Leader 1 would train a Team 1 member on day 1, Team Leader 2 would train an associate of Team 2 on the next day, and so on.

An HR representative would spend time with the group every day for 2 weeks. This representative would arrive before the second period, talk with the trainer and associate in training, answer any questions or address any problems, and so on. The representative would also observe the entire training session and then discuss the session with the trainer and associate to determine how to improve the process and evaluate whether or not the program was accomplishing its goals.

The Nuts and Bolts of Each Training Session

The first session covered Quadrant 1. The goal of the first session was to let the associate absorb knowledge of the process by watching, asking questions, listening, and participating (hands-on) in some part of the process. The trainer talked with the associate about common safety concerns and appropriate responses to safety problems or emergencies. The trainer would then discuss typical quality problems the associate might encounter as well as appropriate responses if such problems arose.

To initiate the hands-on component of the session, the trainer would begin doing the job, with the associate in a position where he or she could watch. Associates were encouraged to ask questions about what the trainer was doing. Occasionally, the trainer would give the associate one or two parts to assemble, gradually involving the associate in the actual process. The goal of the second session was to train the associate to complete an entire process by the end of the period (Quadrant 2). The trainer monitored the associate's activity through the entire period, making sure that every step was completed properly. The trainer would intervene if the associate encountered difficulty, but the associate was expected to perform the entire process, with zero defects.

During the third session (Quadrant 3), the trainer would assist the associate to achieve the skill level needed to complete a process to takt time. The trainer would stay at the station the entire period to ensure that standardized work procedures were followed. The objective here was to allow the associate to gain confidence and speed while, at the same time, completing the job correctly.

Rudrey liked this hands-on, on-the-job training method because it promoted good communication between associates and team leaders. It also provides a training method that did not jeopardize quality.

Certain processes were exceptionally complex, and Rudrey realized that not every session would go smoothly. In such cases, associates were not likely to master every aspect of a process during a single period, and training at the same level would continue until the associate reached the necessary level of proficiency.

This system of training had another advantage: It demonstrated the power of progressing from one level to the next. Thus, associates who "arrived" at Quadrant 4 were not surprised at being told it was not the end of the journey but a stage in the quest for continuous improvement. Associates that reached Quadrant 4 possessed ample knowledge to assist in the continuous improvement of the process and standardized work.

Tweaking the System

Rudrey's HR originally planned to give each group enough quadrant sheets for every associate to undergo training at every workstation. In the process of developing these sheets, however, HR realized that there would be a lot of unnecessary duplication and overlapping and decided to create a generic version of the quadrant sheet, which trainers could modify and tailor as needed. Trainers had some leeway on this, but the basic structure and sequence of items was retained. See Figure 8-11.

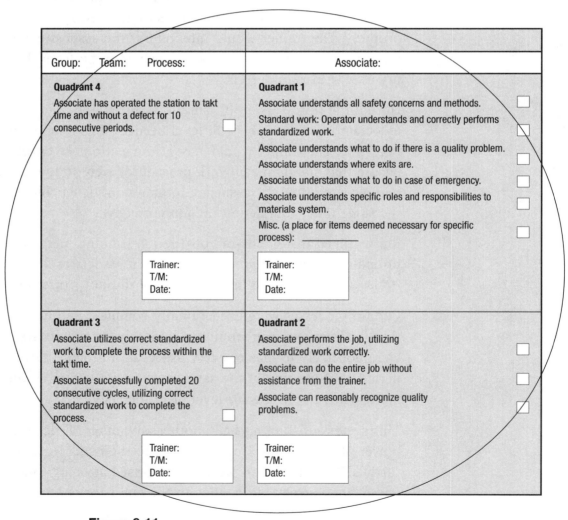

Group: Team: Process:	Associate:
Quadrant 4 Associate has operated the station to takt time and without a defect for 10 consecutive periods. ☐	**Quadrant 1** Associate understands all safety concerns and methods. ☐ Standard work: Operator understands and correctly performs standardized work. ☐ Associate understands what to do if there is a quality problem. ☐ Associate understands where exits are. ☐ Associate understands what to do in case of emergency. ☐ Associate understands specific roles and responsibilities to materials system. ☐ Misc. (a place for items deemed necessary for specific process): _____ ☐
Trainer: T/M: Date:	Trainer: T/M: Date:
Quadrant 3 Associate utilizes correct standardized work to complete the process within the takt time. ☐ Associate successfully completed 20 consecutive cycles, utilizing correct standardized work to complete the process. ☐	**Quadrant 2** Associate performs the job, utilizing standardized work correctly. ☐ Associate can do the entire job without assistance from the trainer. ☐ Associate can reasonably recognize quality problems. ☐
Trainer: T/M: Date:	Trainer: T/M: Date:

Figure 8-11.

To ensure that trainers were training correctly, HR instituted a system of checks: An HR representative visited every group in the facility every week, spoke with the group leader and team leaders about on-the-job training, and reviewed the training matrices and calendar to ascertain whether or not training was happening every day. Human Resources also monitored the training for one period to see whether any additional tweaking was necessary.

Summing Up

- Who needs to be trained? The associates (team members).

- Who needs to train? The team leader.

- What needs to be trained? Now, every workstation in the team; in the future, the group.

- When does the training need to begin? Immediately and on a small scale.

- Where does the training happen? On the production floor.

- How are the team members trained? One at a time, on the production floor, following the training matrix (quadrants).

CHAPTER 9

Developing Group Leaders (Supervisors)

Production supervisors at Rudrey went through all of the training described in the previous chapters of this book (Chapter 2 summarizes these training sessions; Chapters 3 to 7 discuss each in more detail). Because supervisory roles change dramatically in a lean transformation, Rudrey management felt that supervisors and team leaders needed additional training to help them deal with their new responsibilities and effectively support the lean initiative.

Such additional training is standard practice in most companies going lean. Some of the training is straightforward and can be handled in the scope of a brief conversation. Other supervisory training requires a more structured approach. At Rudrey, the training evolved as supervisor-specific workshops with a dual purpose: 1) to show supervisors how their jobs would were going to change, and 2) to show how to supervise a lean workforce. The plant manager attended each workshop session. (Note that the term "supervisor" and "group leader" are used interchangeably throughout the remainder of the chapter.)

Goals for the Training

Goals for group leader training at Rudrey were as follows:

- Explain the importance of the supervisor's role and the difference between past practices and future practices.
- Explain standardized work and auditing.
- Explain and provide production status boards.
- Explain the role of group leaders in continuous improvement.

The Nuts and Bolts of Group Leader Training

As noted above, Rudrey's team leaders and production supervisors completed the same training as the company's associates. Now it was time to focus on teaching supervisors the new skills and concepts that they would need to support the change initiative. From the start, Rudrey's trainer adopted an approach that was learner friendly as well as instructive.

A Day in the Life of Two Supervisors

The initial workshop session was designed to explain the difference in past practices and future practices and to show that Rudrey management understood the differences between the two. This was the first time that the Rudrey trainer had only production supervisors in the classroom, and she tailored her delivery to accommodate her audience. She began with a short presentation called "A Day in the Life of Two Supervisors," dividing the supervisors' day into eight sections: preparation for the day's activities, the line start up, before first break, around 9:00 A.M., between 9:00 and 11:00 A.M., lunch, after lunch, and after last break.

The left-hand side of the slides shown during this presentation contained a description of what a traditional supervisor in a mass manufacturing environment does during each of these sections of the workday. The right-hand side of the slide described what a lean production supervisor does during each section. (See Figure 9-1.)

Preparation for the Day's Activities

Traditional Supervisor	*Lean Supervisor*
• Reads log book from opposite shift.	• Reads log book from opposite shift.
• Records first job number.	• Walks each operation for visual confirmation.
• Monitors screen for manpower updates.	• Checks min. and max. levels.
• Determines whether or not the line can run.	• Reviews quality charts from opposite shift.
• Worries about what the boss is going to say.	• Observes for proper startup.
	• Has training matrix ready.
	• Holds brief team leader meeting.

Figure 9-1.

Preparation for the day's activities was the first section, and the trainer explained that the most significant effort on the part of the traditional supervisor is to determine whether or not the line can run, that is, whether he or she has enough parts, people, and properly running machinery. On the other hand, in a lean environment, the supervisor goes through a series of visual checks and startup procedures, has a meeting with team leaders, and then begins the day.

The trainer then discussed what occurs when the line starts. The traditional supervisor still works on labor requirements and checks on parts to make sure that he or she will be able to run the product. The lean supervisor utilizes a training matrix to see which associates can be moved, if need be, and verbally communicates with each team member. (See Figure 9-2.) The lean supervisor also uses this time frame to audit standard work.

The Line Starts

Traditional Supervisor	Lean Supervisor
• Works on manpower requirements.	• Relies on visual control.
• Checks on material shortages.	• Moves manpower accordingly.
• Deals with personnel problems.	• Observes process flow.
• Tries to check on quality.	• Engages in verbal communication with team members.
• Takes trip to the end of the line.	• Checks quality control systems.
• Worries about what the boss is going to say.	• Has training matrix ready.

Figure 9-2.

Morning before first break normally begins with the traditional supervisor still chasing parts so that his or her line can run. The lean supervisor, on the other hand, uses this valuable time to check on progress and quality, and sometimes works to cross-train on the processes himself. See Figure 9-3.

The next section discussed was the 9:00 A.M. break. During this break, the traditional supervisor attends a managers' meeting. Focused on getting through the meeting, the supervisor does not yet know how

Morning Before First Break

Traditional Supervisor

- Chases missing parts.

- Tries to accommodate breaks for medical, restroom, and other personal reasons.

- Answers quality inspection requests.

- Starts to tag scrap (always trying to charge back to someone else and not looking at root cause).

- Worries about what the boss is going to say.

Lean Supervisor

- Reviews quality charts.

- Reviews cost charts.

- Checks standardize work: verification.

- Checks information center for status.

- Reviews problem processes.

- Checks with other groups.

- Works on the line for cross training.

- Monitors groups work.

Figure 9-3.

the line is running with regard to quality and productivity. (The trainer pointed out that this lack of information is disturbing, but it is the result of a poor system, not a poor supervisor.) The lean supervisor, on the other hand, goes on break and reviews the charts for production, quality, cost, and other aspects of the line work, which are posted in the break room. He then sits in on a short safety meeting led by a team member. See Figure 9-4.

Around 9:00 A.M.

Traditional Supervisor

- Break: Attends morning meeting with supervisors.

- Watches group go in all different directions.

- Realizes that group has no idea where they are with regards to quality and cost.

- Thinks "How am I going to get that done?"

- Starts to worry about audit.

- Has no real idea how the line is running.

Lean Supervisor

- Goes on break.

- Attends short 5-minute safety meeting.

- Sees most of the team members in break area.

- In the break area, reads charts on quality, production, attendance, and reviews cross-training charts with others.

- Attends short meeting with team leaders to determine cross-training schedule.

- Manager is looking for support and education.

Figure 9-4.

The presentation continued with the 9:00 to 11:00 A.M. time frame after the break. The traditional supervisor wonders what is going to happen next and puts out fires. He or she is still chasing parts and is now monitoring inventory levels as well. The lean supervisor spends this time monitoring different areas under his or her supervision for improvement opportunities. See Figure 9-5.

After Break

Traditional Supervisor

- Wonders what is going to happen next.
- Walks around.
- Responds to quality defect.
- Puts out fires.
- Attends to people's needs.
- Worries about lunch break.
- Runs out of parts.
- Responds to customer complaint.
- Starts thinking of explanation for the boss.
- Talks to operator about defect.

Lean Supervisor

- Observes at the end of the section for improvements that can be made.
- Checks quality at the end of the section.
- Updates quality charts.
- Does problem solving.

Figure 9-5.

During lunch, the traditional supervisor has problems with associates leaving the line early. Sometimes the line stops, and the supervisor does not know why. The lean area's associates complete the process they are working on and then go to lunch. Information about the productivity, quality, cost, and performance are displayed on a screen in the break area. See Figure 9-6.

After lunch, the traditional supervisor is again concerned about being able to run the line. Part levels must be checked, employees coming back late from lunch must be covered for, and so on. The lean supervisor, on the other hand, checks systems for proper startup and then goes to work on the line to keep his or her skill levels sharp. See Figure 9-7.

In describing the last break period, the trainer noted that traditional supervisors can seldom point to the day's accomplishments; having

---

Lunch

Traditional Supervisor

- Notices that employees leave the line early.
- Has no idea where they stopped.
- Has no visual control.

Lean Supervisor

- Notes that team members complete their processes.
- Sees that line stops at fixed position.
- Knows that information on plant and its performance is available on information screen.

Figure 9-6.

After Lunch

Traditional Supervisor

- Is concerned about being able to run the line.
- Answers call from boss.
- Checks audit: Work system back problems.
- Experiences more problems.

Lean Supervisor

- Checks for proper start-up.
- Monitors group activities.
- Updates charts.
- Goes on the line to keep skill level high.
- Performs 6S audit.
- Does standardized work audits.
- Does material audit (pull signals).

Figure 9-7.

spent most of the day chasing parts, they often go home feeling exhausted. The lean supervisor updates charts, checks each process, completes the logbook, and organizes the area before leaving the plant. See Figure 9-8.

In concluding this presentation, the trainer emphasized that the differences in the way the two supervisors did their jobs and handled their activities during the day were shaped and influenced by the environments in which they worked and the systems utilized within those environments. The lean system allowed the lean supervisor to supervise; the traditional environment forced the traditional supervisor to chase parts and people and put out fires.

Last Break

Traditional Supervisor

- Survives the day.
- Tries to accommodate relief time for people.
- Explains a quality defect.
- Returns call from the boss.
- Starts log book for next shift.
- Chases material: out of parts.
- Experiences no accomplishments for the day.
- Watches people working ahead to get off 2 minutes early.

Lean Supervisor

- Attends quality review.
- Plans for tomorrow.
- Updates charts.
- Problem solves.
- Checks each process.
- Completes log book.
- Has a 6S supervisor desk.

Figure 9-8.

At this point, the trainer asked the supervisors to answer a question: "Why are you here?" Most of the supervisors could not answer. The trainer then explained that at Rudrey, as at other lean facilities, supervisors are the informational link between management and associates. She added that Rudrey supervisors play a vital role in the development, improvement, and success of the Rudrey Production System. This, however, meant that supervisors would have to understand the changes that would affect their jobs.

The changes would not involve more responsibilities (something that frequently occurred in the old days) but different responsibilities. In some cases, in fact, there would be fewer responsibilities: Supervisors would no longer be concerned with the time-consuming tasks of scheduling or part chasing.

Rudrey supervisors who had lived through other change initiatives were skeptical, and the trainer explained that one of the reasons previous changes had been so difficult was lack of management involvement. She stressed that Rudrey management was committed to the change, would provide support throughout the change process, and would address any problems supervisors faced. The workshop trainer then discussed key issues that would help supervisors do their jobs under the new system.

Staffing Issues

Rudrey HR understood that job-changing policy (also called bumping) had been impeding the Operations part of the business. Every month, senior associates could bump associates with less seniority and move into their areas and jobs almost at will. Rudrey HR saw that this policy was detrimental to the flow of product. Every time someone changed areas, there was a learning curve to contend with because the associate taking over the job had to get up to speed. Human Resources informed supervisors that future job changing would be limited to once a year, a dramatic change that would reduce the disruption in flow while still allowing associates to work in different areas and learn new skills.

Another staffing problem, discussed in Chapter 8 of this book, was lack of information on who was trained on which processes. The training matrix developed by HR would now allow supervisors to see quickly which operators were capable of doing which jobs.

Standardized Work

Standardized work is doing the same thing every time. This is essential for any company aspiring to achieve world-class status and also essential to consistent quality production. For this reason, Rudrey management made standardized work an important part of the supervisors' training session. Figure 9-9 outlines the essential components of standardized work.

Standardized Work

- Doing the same thing every time
- Essential to quality
- Essential to productivity

There can be no improvements without standards to improve on!

Figure 9-9

The trainer stressed that supervisors would not develop the initial standardized work. This would be done by the industrial engineers, continuous improvement teams, and the Lean Coordinator, with input from the value-added associates. Supervisors would, however, make sure that standardized work was followed. They would also be responsible for improving the standardized work, through the auditing process with employee input. The trainer then presented templates for standardized worksheets for the floor (see Figures 9-10 and 9-11), one for the entire area and one for each individual workstation.

The trainer then explained the auditing process. Every supervisor, along with management, would set aside a time of day for auditing work standards, a time during which no meetings or other scheduled events could occur. The team decided that the best time for this was 8:00 A.M. to 9:00 A.M., just before the daily morning break. Within this time frame, supervisors would review the work standards and make sure employees were adhering to them. Managers, including the plant manager, would audit at the same time.

Standardized Work Chart at Area Level

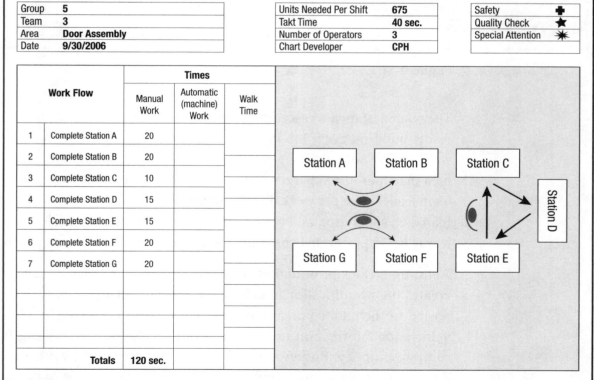

Figure 9-10.

Standardized Work Chart at Process (Station) Level

Group	5	
Team	3	
Area	**Door Assembly**	
Station	A	

Units Needed Per Shift	**675**
Processing Time	**20 sec.**
Beginning Step	**Rt. Dr.**
Ending Step	**Mv. Pt.**

Date	
Safety	✚
Quality Check	★
Special Attention	✳

	Work Elements	Manual Work	Automatic (machine) Work	Walk Time
1	Attach Right Door	5		
2	Attach Left Door	5		
3	Attach Fitting	2		
4	Attach Clip	3		
5	Secure Clip	2		
6	Move part	3		
	Totals	**20 sec.**		

This area of the chart is used to visually explain the work elements and any items that need special attention. This can be done by hand drawing, computer drawing, or digital pictures, etc.

Figure 9-11.

The team designed a cascading system of audits that began with the team leader auditing every job in his or her team every shift. The supervisor would audit one job along with the team leader during every shift. The area manager (the supervisor's boss) would audit with the supervisor and team leader once per week. Finally, once a month, the plant manager, area manager, supervisor, and team leader would audit the same job, to ensure it was being performed correctly and to look for improvement potential.

Auditing creates information flow between levels of management and creates opportunities for improvement throughout the facility. When posted in the audited area, the audit sheet is not a "gotcha" tool, but a vehicle for information flow and a way to make sure everything is running properly. Rudrey utilized the standardized audit worksheet illustrated in Figure 9-12 and trained the supervisors how to conduct the audit and document what they found.

Group or Area Audited   Station Name
                                         or Number

Month & Year of Audit   Auditor
                                         Initials

Auditor to fill out shaded areas   Date of
                                         Audit

Are the standard work charts up to date?

Are the standard work charts visible?

Is the cell or line staffed properly?

Are the walk patterns being followed?

Is the work being performed to the station chart?

Are parts presentation devices in their proper location?

Are the parts presentation devices used correctly?

Are the production targets updated to the posted plan?

Is the production reporting board being updated?

Is Management auditing the production reporting boards?

Note: Whenever an "X" is placed in a box, the corrective action should be taken before the end of the shift by the supervisor

Comments:

Audit Procedure

1. Check one job per day per team.

2. Check different person on the job each week.

3. Check person for 10 straight cycles.

4. If person checked is following Standardized Work, place an "O" in the designated block.

5. If person audited is NOT following Standardized Work, place an "X" in the box & list the cause in the comments section.

Adapted from *Creating Continuous Flow* by Mike Rother and Rick Harris. (Cambridge, MA: LEI, 2003). p. 94.

Figure 9-12.

The final part of standardized work deals with how supervisors manage their areas. This is the labor linearity part of standardized work. Standardized work should happen at the process level, cellular or manufacturing area level, and the management level—labor linearity deals with the cellular or manufacturing area portion of this schematic. Cells or manufacturing areas are set up so that they can function with one associate, a fully staffed team, or anything in between. Labor linearity is set up so that the supervisor can fully grasp what happens when an associate is added to or subtracted from the floor at any given time. This gives the supervisor the knowledge and flexibility to react promptly and efficiently to customer demand.

At Rudrey, industrial engineers and Lean Coordinators develop labor linearity documentation, with input from the supervisor. The labor linearity chart, shown in Figure 9-13, details the number of associates required to produce a given number of parts. It is an integral planning tool for the supervisor, because it shows exactly how many people need to be working in the area to produce the number of parts that customers want.

Labor Linearity

- 1 operator   = 200 parts
- 2 operators = 400 parts
- 3 operators = 600 parts
- 4 operators = 800 parts
- 5 operators = 900 parts

Figure 9-13

Management Time frame and the Production Status Board

"Management time frame" refers to how often you check to see how an area is running. When the trainer asked Rudrey supervisors how often they do this, the answers ranged from once a shift to once a day, with most indicating they did this work at the end of a shift. When the trainer asked how they did this, most supervisors answered that they approached the task by counting parts and then counting parts without defects. Based on what they found, they determined whether the shift or the day was productive or not.

The problem with this approach is that a one-shift management time-frame makes it difficult to fix a problem that occurs near the beginning of the shift. There are no systems in place to see a problem until the end of the shift (or the entire day). Rudrey's solution to this was to introduce production status boards, shown in Figure 9-14.

Team:		Team Leader:		Group Leader:		
Time	Plan	Actual	Comments		Group Leader	Area Manager
7:00–8:00	200					
8:00–9:00	200					
9:15–10:00	150					
10:00–11:00	200					
11:30–12:00	100					
12:00–1:15	250					
1:30–2:30	200					
2:30–3:30	200					
Total	1300					

Figure 9-14

A production status board accomplishes three things for a manufacturing area. The first is that it provides the hourly associates with expectations for the day. Expectations are calculated by utilizing the standardized work labor linearity charts and customer demand, which comes from the Materials department (discussed in the "The Supervisor's Role in Continuous Flow and Materials Delivery Systems" section later in this chapter). The second objective that a production status board accomplishes is that it gives associates a tool for letting the supervisor know when someone sees a problem or an opportunity for improvement. Finally, a production status board gives the supervisor a nudge to visit his or her area every hour and look at the production status boards: The supervisor has to initial the board every hour.

With a production status board in place, management time frame goes from an entire shift (or day) to 1 hour. Now if a problem happens at the beginning of the shift, the supervisor can take necessary action to fix the problem within the hour.

The trainer emphasized the importance of fixing problems as they arise. In the past, upper management accepted (even sometimes encouraged) putting a band-aid on problems as a quick fix, with the idea that the problem could be properly fixed sometime in the future. If a machine broke down, for example, it was easier to have the operator manually reset the machine each time instead of going through the process of getting capital to fix the machine. In the long run, this approach wasted time and, in some cases, increased the cost of repairs. The workshop trainer explained that Rudrey management found this approach unacceptable and assured the supervisors that management would now fix machines and other flow disruptions promptly.

The trainer indicated, however, that this new policy had to be a two-way street. A supervisor spotting a problem on the status board could not simply initial the board and walk away. This would make the board useless: Management could not fix a problem if it did know about it, and associates would soon lose interest in documenting problems that no one bothered to fix.

Production status boards benefit supervisors because they provide clear goals. With the boards, supervisors can focus on making sure that hourly production matches the production plan, so that the flow of the facility is smooth and efficient.

Supervisors and Workplace Organization

The next portion of the training session was workplace organization. Workplace organization is a topic that is not difficult to explain (see Chapter 4), because most of the learning comes from implementation. The 6S process is the same for everyone in the facility: It is a well-defined series of steps that every employee, facility-wide, can utilize to organize an area.

Supervisors had already participated on the core training on 6S; the workshop trainer now focused on the daily 6S audit. Supervisors were told they needed to audit their areas every day. Everyone would use a standard form (like the one shown in Figure 9-15) and post audits so that everyone in a given area could see them.

Rudrey 6S Audit Form

Date: _____

Area: _____

Auditor: _____

*If No is checked on any item, the area automatically recieves a 1 for that "S."
**For each NO, a corrective action needs to be developed and completed.
***Scores are 1–5 for each "S," Area Score is the total of the 6 "S" scores.

	Yes	No	Score for "S"
Sort			
Does everything in the area belong in the area?	____	____	_____
Is the red tag area well identified?	____	____	_____
Is there evidence that the red tag area is being utilized?	____	____	_____
Straighten			
Does every item in the area have a place?	____	____	_____
Is every place for an item identified?	____	____	_____
Are visual controls utilized to identify each place (tape, paint, etc.)?	____	____	_____
Is the tape on the floor in good shape?	____	____	_____
Shine			
Is the area clean?	____	____	_____
Are the machines in the area clean?	____	____	_____
Is the floor swept?	____	____	_____
Standardize			
Is the area following the facility standards?	____	____	_____
Sustain			
Are past audits posted in the area?	____	____	_____
Is there evidence that the audits are being used to improve?	____	____	_____
Safety			
Does the area appear to be free of obvious safety hazards?	____	____	_____
Are safety meetings being conducted on a regular basis?	____	____	_____
Is there evidence that open safety issues are being addressed?	____	____	_____
Area Score			_____

*5 = Outstanding; 4 = Above Expectations; 3 = Acceptable; 2 = Not Acceptable; 1 = Action Needed

Figure 9-15.

A 6S audit is simple and does not take long, but it is a wonderful tool for maintaining a clean and organized working environment. If something wrong appears on the audit, the supervisor needs to take corrective action. The trainer stressed that audits *cannot be delegated to someone else: they are the supervisor's responsibility.*

Supervisors and Value Stream Maps

When designing the training session on value stream mapping (see Chapter 5), Rudrey's HR department worked closely with Operations and the Lean Coordinator to determine who would draw the value stream maps. Everyone realized that if supervisors were going to draw the maps, they would require extensive training and HR determined that, for the time being, the production supervisors' time would be better spent on the implementation of other initiatives. The consensus was that engineers and upper management would continue to draw the maps and, for this reason, supervisors did not receive additional training on this subject.

The Supervisor's Role in Continuous Flow and Materials Delivery Systems

In the past, Rudrey production supervisors were not really supervisors. They were schedulers and part chasers. In fact, the old method of scheduling at Rudrey was jokingly referred to as, "the place-and-chase method"—someone would place the schedule, and then the supervisors would chase the parts and the people necessary to produce the product. Supervisors could not do much to improve the system; they just tried to survive each day and hoped the next day would be better. The real problem was that "the system" in place was no system at all: There were no clear-cut standards to improve upon.

In the supervisory training for continuous flow and materials delivery routes, supervisors were told they would no longer be scheduling part deliveries. In addition, supervisors would no longer be scheduling production. Both of these tasks would become the responsibility of the Materials department.

With this change, the supervisors' job description changed dramatically. Scheduling and chasing parts, which often consumed half a day or more, had suddenly disappeared from the list. No longer burdened with these responsibilities, supervisors could now be supervisors and use their time to audit processes, fix problems, and communicate with associates about how to improve processes.

In the past, supervisors received a production schedule (like the ones illustrated in Figure 9-16). They were the only individuals who received this information, therefore it provided a sense of importance; if someone wanted to know what to run next, he or she had to ask the supervisor because there was no other way to obtain this information. Some supervisors liked the set up: The exclusive knowledge made them feel important and indispensable.

Under the new system, Materials would schedule each value stream. Moreover, the value stream map was radically different (see Figure 9-17).

Supervisors no longer needed to have an elaborate schedule, because when one process pulled something from its market, what was removed was replenished. Figures 9-18 and 9-19 show scheduling controlled by a push system (the old way) and scheduling controlled by a pull system (the lean way), respectively.

The trainer then explained to the supervisors how this would affect their roles. The explanation focused on the fact that Rudrey management wanted the supervisors to play a significant role in the continuous improvement of the facility. To do this, they could not be strapped by having to schedule their areas. Instead, they would create and facilitate a partnership between the Operations and Materials departments. Operations would produce product scheduled by the Materials department; the Materials department would level, balance, and schedule the facility. In connection with this, Operations would strive to achieve excellent quality and efficiency; Materials would move material efficiently and correctly. Both would focus on continuous improvement. See Figure 9-20.

At this point, the trainer asked the supervisors, "How many of you have ever been scheduled to produce product without having the parts to make it?" Every supervisor in the room raised his or her hand. The inefficient outcome was obvious: no product made and supervisors having to run other parts until the correct parts arrived.

The trainer then asked, "How many of you have ever run out of a part during the middle of a production run?" Once again, everyone's

112

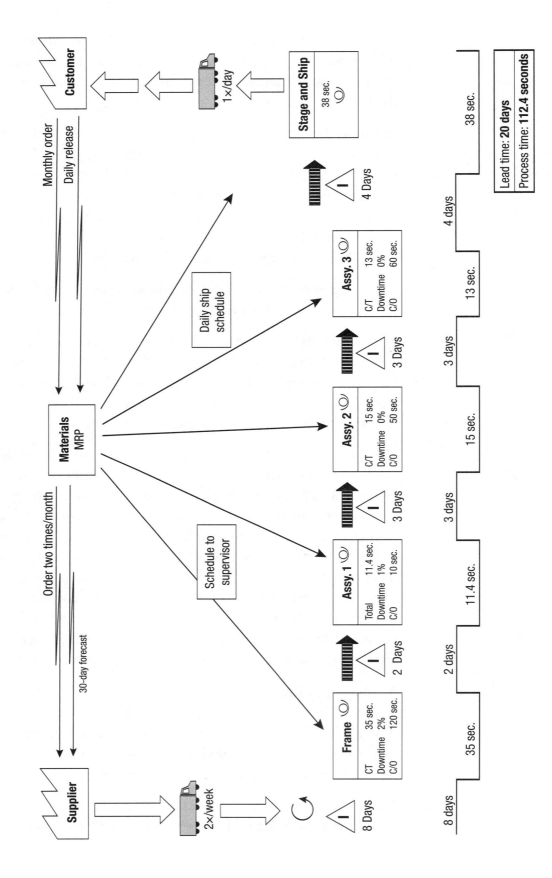

Figure 9-16.

113

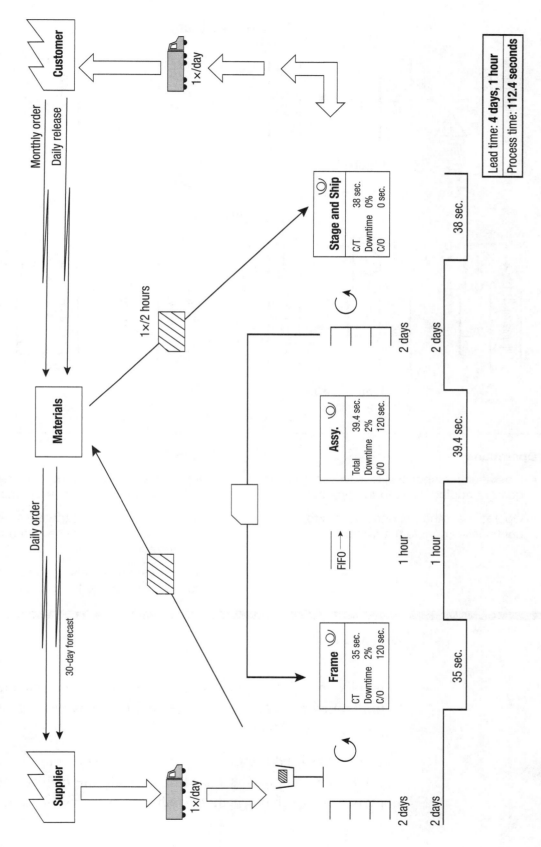

Customer

Monthly order

Daily release

1×/day

Materials

Daily order

30-day forecast

Supplier

1×/day

2 days

1×/2 hours

Stage and Ship

C/T	38 sec.
Downtime	0%
C/0	0 sec.

Assy.

Total	39.4 sec.
Downtime	2%
C/0	120 sec.

Frame

CT	35 sec.
Downtime	2%
C/0	120 sec.

FIFO →

2 days

1 hour

35 sec.

1 hour

39.4 sec.

2 days

2 days

38 sec.

Lead time: **4 days, 1 hour**
Process time: **112.4 seconds**

Figure 9-17.

Push (before Lean)

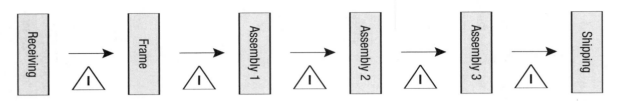

Figure 9-18.

Future

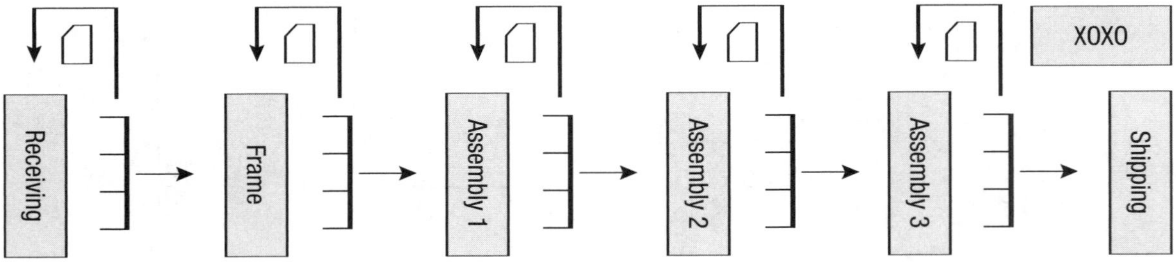

Figure 9-19.

Operations

- Operations' responsibility is to become very good at adding value to the product.
- Operations' other responsibility is to continually improve the system.

Materials

- It is the Materials department's responsibility to level balance and schedule the facility.
- It is the Materials department's responsibility to make sure parts are delivered on time in the correct quantities.
- It is also the Materials department's job to continually improve the process.

Figure 9-20.

hand went up. Supervisors know this inefficient outcome, too: an unplanned changeover and a second disruptive changeover when the parts finally arrive.

The trainer used these questions to underscore why the Materials department had been selected to schedule the facility and deliver the parts to make that schedule. Under the new system, Materials could never schedule the assembly of a product without also giving the line the parts with which to make it.

The trainer noted that, even though the supervisors were going to be hands-off on the Materials side, they would have other, different responsibilities. They would, for example, play a role in the purchased parts markets and work in process markets, where their main responsibility would be monitoring (auditing) work-in-process markets, keeping them clean and organized, and ensuring that parts were always where they were needed. In addition, supervisors would have to be vigilant about what was being produced (only product that has been pulled from the market); the system would fail if an area produced the wrong product or the wrong quantities. As for the purchased parts market, the supervisors were cautioned about two specific things: Parts in purchased parts markets were off-limits and back-up boxes hidden in the area or locked in a desk drawer were a thing of the past. It would now be the responsibility of the Materials department to control inventory and make sure that supervisors did not run out of product. Supervisors did not need to guard against outages by taking from purchased parts or by keeping emergency stashes.

The trainer emphasized that pull signals were vital to the success of the material handling system and that ensuring the accuracy and proper use of pull signals was the biggest responsibility that supervisors would have to the Materials department. The pull signals tell Materials what an area needs. If the signals are mishandled, someone will run out of parts.

The final responsibility for supervisors was to assure that the aisle ways were always clear (see Figure 9-21). Drivers were on a timed delivery route and could not do their jobs if they could not easily drive through an area's aisle ways.

Continuous Improvement and Supervisors

The management team at Rudrey meant what they said about the production supervisors' role in the continuous improvement of the facility. Because the supervisors at Rudrey were no longer responsible for scheduling and chasing parts, they would have time to supervise. One of their new responsibilities was auditing standardized work and implementing

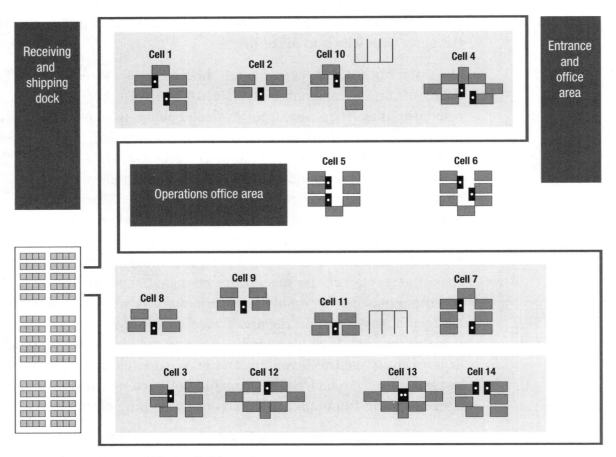

Figure 9-21.

improvements through the employee suggestion program. Each supervisor would serve as a point person for employee suggestions in his or her area. In the past, employee suggestions had been underutilized, misused, and underappreciated. Often, the suggestions never reached the right people. In Rudrey's new lean environment, supervisors would become the right people, listen to suggestions, and utilize them in continuous improvement endeavors.

When this idea was first discussed, the supervisors were not very enthusiastic. The trainer quickly reminded them that this was a way that they could play a significant role in the improvement of processes and, reminded them that they no longer had the responsibility of scheduling and part chasing. She emphasized that fielding suggestions was not just a way to fill time, but a strategy that could yield excellent results. To accomplish this, however, supervisors would have to take ownership of the employee-suggestion program, encouraging ideas, evaluating *all* ideas, and putting the best ideas into action. They would solicit suggestions by talking with associates and write the suggestions on a standard form (see Figure 9-22).

Rudrey Employee Suggestion Program

Name: _____ Group: _____

Group Leader: _____ Date Received: _____

Suggestion: (Detailed explanations and pictures if necessary)

_____
_____
_____
_____
_____
_____
_____
_____
_____
_____
_____
_____
_____
_____
_____
_____
_____
_____
_____

Approved: [   ] Project implementation date: _____

Denied: [   ] Detailed reason for denial:_____

(Use separate page if necessary)

Figure 9-22.

So, going forward, supervisors would be responsible for all employee suggestions in their areas.

Supervisors would then evaluate each suggestion and talk as soon as possible with the appropriate people: Industrial Engineering, the Materials department, plant management, and so on. The goal was to ensure that a suggestion would either be accepted or denied within one week, with the supervisor informing the associate of the decision in writing. The memo to the associate would include a reason for denial or a projected date of implementation. If the idea was accepted, the supervisor would be responsible for seeing that it was implemented.

Summing Up

- Explain the difference between supervising in a traditional manufacturing environment and in a lean manufacturing environment.

- Define new roles for the supervisor, and explain previous roles and how they are no longer valid (scheduling and chasing parts).

- Be absolutely sure that the plant manager, the area manager, and an HR representative play a major role in training.

- Explain and give examples of how supervisors are the catalysts for driving continuous improvement throughout the facility.

- Break information into one-hour training blocks to keep in line with the facility training plan.

CHAPTER 10

Continually Improving Your Workforce Through New Hires, Promotions, and Ongoing Training

After you develop a standard method of training employees at your facility, you need to continue to train new employees, conduct periodic new training, and offer more in-depth training of existing employees, as needed. Previous chapters addressed how the HR department at Rudrey developed a standard method of training current employees in the Rudrey Production System and implementation. Rudrey also developed a standard method of training the operators on the floor so that they could perform every process in their team. Rudrey's HR was now charged with developing a plan to continuously improve the Rudrey Production System by training new hires and providing new and/or more in-depth training for existing employees.

In addition, Rudrey management realized the importance of their future leadership and wanted to develop solid lean leadership from within. This meant focusing on the team leader and group leader positions.

Training New Hires

Rudrey began by rethinking the way it handled its new-hire orientation, as well as new-hire training. The company wanted to develop new-hire training sessions along the same lines it had developed the lean manufacturing training sessions described in Chapters 3 through 8.

Rudrey already had a great deal of training material for new hires. That material was almost identical to the material used to train the employees on lean manufacturing implementation (Lean 101). However, because lean thinking was now part of the Rudrey culture, there was no need to call new-hire training "lean"—the company decided to call it Rudrey Manufacturing 101.

Exercise

How long does it take a new hire at your facility to effectively add value on the floor as a member of the team? Why do you feel it takes this long? How much value-added time is lost at your facility because newly hired employees begin working on the production floor before they are ready?

Rudrey was determined to provide Operations with associates who understood the Rudrey Production System and could provide value quickly. To do this, the company developed a new-hire path. The following is a day-by-day plan that Rudrey developed and utilized to transfer newly hired employees to the production floor so that they could begin adding value quickly and efficiently.

Day 1

On the first day, new employees attended a standard new-hire orientation, during which they learned about work hours, benefits, and so on. After day one, a system of acclimating new associates to RPS began in earnest.

Day 2

On Day 2, each newly hired employee met with a Human Resources professional who first inquired whether or not there were any questions about Day 1. Once any questions were handled, the new employee was introduced to the training matrix discussed in Chapter 8 and advised what to expect during Period 2,[1] which entailed getting acquainted with the floor and with the area team leader. The team leader would then begin training the new associates in the manner discussed in Chapter 8.

---

1. The work day is broken into four periods. Period 1 is start up until 1st break. Period 2 is end of 1st break to lunch. Period 3 is end of lunch to 2nd break. Period 4 is end of 2nd break to the end of the day.

The goal of this first period of training, essentially the new hire's first official workstation, was to get the employee through the first quadrant of the training matrix. Following this session, the new employee returned to the classroom for Period 3—the Rudrey Manufacturing 101 training module. In Period 4, the employee returned to the floor to continue training with the team leader at the same workstation as before.

By utilizing this method, Rudrey HR provided a good mix of classroom instruction and on-the-job training. This method got new employees out on the floor, but guarded against the problems of the past, when newly hired employees attended a standard orientation session and were then sent to the production floor to sink or swim. In Rudrey's new method, these employees were not left to learn on their own; as a result, they became a real asset to Operations because they understood RPS and could perform their assigned jobs within the allotted time. The following is a quick outline of Day 2.

Period 1: Answer any questions from day one, train on the training matrix (see Chapter 8), and explain what can be expected in Period 2.

Period 2: Give on-the-job training at Workstation A, with the goal of having the new hire successfully complete Quadrant 1.[2]

Period 3: Train on Rudrey Manufacturing 101 (Lean 101), answer questions, and prepare for Period 4.

Period 4: Give on-the-job training at Workstation A.

Day 3

Day 3 started the same as Day 2, a meeting with a Human Resources professional. The next step was workplace organization training, followed by on-the-job training on the production floor for Period 2, with the associate assigned to the same workstation, Workstation A, as on Day 1. Period 3 was set aside for handling any questions the associate had about any of the previous days. During Period 4, the new associate went back to Workstation A, with a goal: getting through Quadrant 2.

Period 1: Answer questions from Day 2, train in workplace organization.

---

2. There are four quadrants in the training matrix—see Chapter 8.

Period 2: Give on-the-job training at Workstation A.

Period 3: Review the first 2 days and prepare for Period 4.

Period 4: Give on-the-job training at Workstation A, with a goal of successfully completing Quadrant 2.

Day 4

Day 4 started the same as the 2 previous days, leading into training on value stream maps. The employee spent the remaining three periods of the day on the floor. The goal for the day was getting through Quadrant 3. By achieving this goal, the employee was ready to perform at Workstation A with little assistance and begin adding value to the team.

Period 1: Answer questions from Day 3, train in value stream maps.

Period 2: Give on-the-job training at Workstation A.

Period 3: Give on-the-job training at Workstation A.

Period 4: Give on-the-job training at Workstation A, with a goal of successfully completing Quadrant 3.

Day 5

The same pattern continued on Day 5, but this day's training session was on continuous flow. The goal was to get the newly hired associate to where he or she could operate as an experienced associate—one who no longer required team leader assistance at the workstation. On Day 5, the employee also began training at a new workstation (Workstation B).

Period 1: Answer questions from Day 4, train in continuous flow.

Period 2: Give on-the-job training at Workstation A.

Period 3: Give on-the-job training on Workstation B, with a goal of successfully completing Quadrant 1.

Period 4: Run Workstation A as an experienced associate.

Day 6

Day 6 began the same way as the 5 previous days. At this point, Rudrey expected the new employee to feel comfortable on the production floor.

Period 1: Answer questions from Day 5, new hire should run Workstation A as an experienced associate.

Period 2: Give on-the-job training on Workstation B, with a goal of successfully completing Quadrant 2.

Period 3: Run the process at Workstation A.

Period 4: Give on-the-job training at Workstation B.

Day 7

On Day 7, which followed the same pattern as the preceding days, the goals were to get the newly trained associate through Quadrant 3 on workstation B and provide materials delivery training.

Period 1: Answer questions from Day 6, train in lean materials delivery.

Period 2: Give on-the-job training at Workstation B.

Period 3: Run normal workstation at Workstation A.

Period 4: Give on-the-job training at Workstation B, with a goal of successfully completing Quadrant 3.

Once an employee reached Quadrant 3 at two different workstations and could successfully complete the assigned processes without assistance, he or she was released to Operations to begin work.

It was important that all new hires be qualified in completing two operations so that they could rotate with the rest of the team rather than being stuck doing the same process all day long. Besides avoiding ergonomics problems, this method supported a future goal: quickly training the new employee on *all* jobs in the team. Once this occurred, new associates could do four different jobs throughout the day, a different one each period. The training schedule may seem rigid, but it was a good way to ensure that flow on the manufacturing floor was not disrupted by haphazard new employee learning curves. Rudrey's timed, systematic training approach provided Operations with a capable employee in less than 2 weeks from hire date, a significant improvement over past practices. Moreover, although new hires at Rudrey moved to the floor quickly, they moved with the knowledge and skills needed to complete assigned processes correctly.

Exercise

What is your goal for newly hired employees?

How can you reach that goal?

What can you put in place to ensure that a rigid new-hire training process will be followed?

Who is the best person at your facility to lead this initiative?

What would a rough draft of your new-hire path look like?

Refresher Training

The team at Rudrey addressed the issue of refresher training after they had been going down the lean path about 6 months. They determined that there should be no need for refresher training because the associates utilized what they had learned on a daily basis. Rudrey, however, wanted to reinforce the concept and practice of continuous improvement, and this meant finding a way to keep its associates engaged and consistently on course.

Exercise

How will you be sure that the employees on the floor utilize the training that they have been through? Can they audit? Can they write standard work? What practices can be put in place to ensure that the employees are engaged and consistently using their knowledge?

Offering New Training Sessions

The training sessions described in Chapters 3 through 8 were a significant step toward creating a culture of continuous improvement at Rudrey, but this was only the beginning. Rudrey quickly learned that additional training was necessary if the company wanted to sustain the gains it had already made and build on them by creating and achieving new goals. Approximately a month after the high-priority group was trained (see Chapter 2), the associates in this group were struggling with the concept of standardized work. In weekly meetings, HR, Operations, and the Lean Coordinator identified the need for more training in this area and created a new module on standardized work, one substantially more detailed than what had previously been offered. This session explained standardized work in depth, gave examples from the floor, and provided in-class, hands-on exercises for the associates. By adding training modules as necessary, Rudrey would more effectively meet the needs of Operations and those of its value-added employees.

The Rudrey team saw that the more they trained to keep associates engaged and continually improving processes, the more benefits the company would reap. With this in mind, the team began to look at other areas that could benefit from additional training: the employee suggestion program, quality at the source, and maintenance.

Exercise

How can you encourage value-added associates, team leaders, and supervisors to suggest new training courses?

What process do you envision these new course ideas going through?

Is your facility disciplined enough to stick with an initiative to continually improve the knowledge of the employees? If so, who has to lead the charge? You? If not, what needs to change?

Promoting from Within

At most manufacturing facilities, promotions go from associate to team leader. Traditionally, team leader positions are filled by applicants with the most seniority; no other credentials are necessary. Group leaders (supervisors) are often recruited from outside the company. The chief requirement for group leaders is a college degree; often, manufacturing experience is unnecessary.

Like many other companies, Rudrey did not find it necessary for group leaders or team leaders to have a thorough understanding of the manufacturing system, but this was because there was no real system in place. Once Rudrey began to see the benefits of its lean manufacturing efforts, however, the company also began to see the need for knowledgeable and capable people throughout the facility—not just educated and/or experienced people, but people knowledgeable about the ins and outs of the Rudrey Production System. To fill this need, Rudrey had to change the way positions were filled on the manufacturing floor.

Obviously, a mass overhaul of the current team leaders and group leaders would cause major problems in the manufacturing system, so Rudrey adopted a different approach. No one currently in the team leader position or group leader position would be moved or demoted. When team leaders and group leaders left their positions (whether it was by promotion, retirement, or career change), Rudrey would fill those positions with candidates possessing knowledge that would help improve the system. To do this, however, Rudrey would have to develop a promotion system.

The first step that the Rudrey HR took was to meet with Operations and the Lean Coordinator and review the current practice of filling team leader and group leader positions. This review led to questions that helped them devise an alternative plan. The most important question was, "Who understands the manufacturing system at Rudrey the best?"

The answer was obvious: "The individuals who run the system every day!" This led to the conclusion that group leader positions in the facility should be filled from within the facility, just as team leader positions already were. At the same time, the team realized that Rudrey's current requirements for candidates for both positions had to be changed.

What Is Required in a Team Leader?

Rudrey wanted team leaders who were reliable, good communicators, and willing to learn new processes. In fact, they should have the capacity to learn every job done by the people on their teams. The main reason for this was that team leaders were the designated trainers in their teams; they had to know firsthand what they were training.

Based on these criteria, Rudrey HR developed the following standards for team leader positions:

- **Attendance:** If a team member has a poor attendance record, there is no need for that individual to apply for the team leader position. A team leader has to be reliable, meaning that the group leader needs to be able to count on the team leader being at work on a regular basis.

- **Abilities:** Before a team member can be considered for a team leader position, the team member must be able to do all of the processes in his or her team to takt time.

- **Desire:** In the past, some team members had applied for team leader positions only because of additional pay. Rudrey wanted team leaders who wanted to be team leaders because a dedicated team leader would likely be willing to improve the system more than someone who saw the position as a way to make more money or an entitlement that came with seniority. To help determine who wanted the job for the right reasons, Rudrey decided anyone interested in applying for a team leader position must first successfully complete the team leader preparation program.

Team leader preparation included a review of the manufacturing system, lean manufacturing 101, 6S, value stream maps, continuous flow, and lean materials delivery, along with additional training modules, adjusted to meet the specific needs of team leaders and supplemented with information about specific items team leaders needed to know about various situations and practices. The trainer was the Lean Coordinator for the facility. The outline of the twelve courses designed was as follows:

- What is a team leader?
- What is team leader role in the Rudrey Production System?
- Dealing with the three manufacturing flows (information, material, and people)
- Identifying the seven forms of manufacturing waste
- The team leader and 6S
- Using communications tools
- Using a value stream map

- Work motions, walk patterns, and standardized work
- Training associates in standardized work
- The team leader's role in a material flow system
- Paperwork for the team leader
- Problem solving for team leaders

The team leader preparation program was offered at night (for those who worked days) or during the day (for those who worked nights). Training was scheduled for Tuesdays and Thursdays and lasted for about an hour each day. Team members who met the attendance and ability requirements and that were interested in applying for team leader positions were eligible, but they did not get paid for the training—this was to discourage those who were solely motivated by the prospect of overtime pay. Completing the training took commitment and sacrifice, but completion did not necessarily guarantee a promotion. It simply qualified team members to apply for open team leader positions.

What Is Required in a Group Leader (Supervisor)?

Rudrey also reevaluated the old 4-year-college degree requirement that made a candidate eligible for a position as group leader. Under this requirement, a perspective group leader was interviewed, hired, and then began his or her career in manufacturing. At best, the new group leader's "training" consisted of shadowing another group leader for a week. For this reason alone, newly hired group leaders often had a difficult time adapting to their new environment.

Rudrey's HR knew that experienced team leaders would make better group leaders than outsiders with college degrees but no knowledge of the Rudrey Manufacturing System and met with Operations and the Lean Coordinator to create new standards. The team decided that the processes for becoming a group leader would be much the same as the process for becoming a team leader. Anyone interested in applying for a group leader position had to meet the following requirements:

- **Attendance:** Has been a team leader in good standing with an excellent attendance record.

- **Leadership:** Has shown leadership qualities in the team leader position.

- **Experience:** Has been a team leader for over 1 year.
- **Preparation:** Has completed the group leader preparation program.

A group leader preparation program was devised based on the same cadence as the team leader preparation course (2 days a week for 6 weeks). The program reviewed the manufacturing system and plantwide training and provided additional information on how to deal with different types of issues that group leaders commonly faced.

- What is the group leader role in the Rudrey Production System?
- Setting up a system for communication and delegation
- Dealing with the three manufacturing flows as a group leader (information, material, and people)
- Dealing with the seven forms of manufacturing waste as a group leader
- The group leader and 6S
- Implementing future state value stream maps
- Dealing with disciplinary issues
- Monitoring and improving work motions, walk patterns, and standardized work
- Training in and auditing in standardized work
- The group leader's role in a material flow system
- Paperwork for the group leader
- Problem solving for group leaders

Summing Up

- Develop a standardized, rigid training plan for newly hired associates.
- Continually improve the training program within the facility through new workshops and improving existing workshops.
- Develop a standard plan to promote team leaders and group leaders from within the facility.

Index

About the Authors

Chris Harris, coauthor of the 2005 Shingo Award winning book *Making Materials Flow*, is Vice President of Operations at Harris Lean Systems (www.harrisleansystems.com). Chris first learned about lean manufacturing as a team member on the assembly line at Toyota Motor Manufacturing Kentucky (TMMK) and continued his lean training at Toyota Tsusho America in Georgetown, Kentucky. Because he has also spent time in nonlean (traditional) manufacturing environments as a frontline production supervisor and as a buyer in corporate purchasing, he has a strong theoretical and practical understanding of the difference between lean and nonlean manufacturing environments.

Chris earned a Masters of Business Administration from the Falls School of Business at Anderson University and currently serves on the faculty of the Lean Enterprise Institute. Since 2001, he has worked with Harris Lean Systems to help numerous U.S. organizations implement lean manufacturing systems. Chris also teaches workshops on various lean manufacturing topics at various events and facilities throughout the United States.

Rick Harris has coauthored two Shingo Prize Award winning books: *Creating Continuous Flow* and *Making Materials Flow*, published by James P. Womack and the Lean Enterprise Institute. One of the principal speakers at The Lean Enterprise Institute's monthly lean conference, Rick has also been a featured presenter at the University of Michigan Lean Manufacturing Conference, the European Lean Enterprise Institute Summit, the Maynard Forum, the PERA Conference, the Mississippi State Annual Lean Conference, the European AME Conference, the AME Conference in Chicago, the University of Kentucky Lean Leadership Forum, and the Lean Summit Brazil.

Rick Harris received his lean training while serving as a Manager in Assembly at the Toyota Motor Manufacturing plant in Georgetown, Kentucky (TMMK). He was a member of the startup team at TMMK, where he gained extensive knowledge of the Toyota Production System. During his tenure at TMMK Rick continued his lean learning at the Toyota Tsutsumi Assembly Plant in Toyota City, Japan. Prior to his Toyota experience, he spent 15 years with General Motors. Rick began as a production operator and progressed through the ranks to become a first-line manager at GM. Rick is President of Harris Lean Systems Incorporated, (HLS, Inc.). Harris Lean Systems has lean practitioners in over 180 facilities throughout the world, assisting over 50 different companies implement lean production systems.